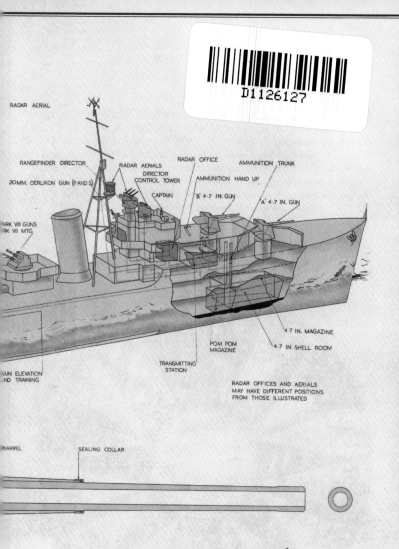

RADAR AERIAL

RANGEFINDER DIRECTOR

20MM. OERLIKON GUN (P AND S)

RADAR AERIALS
DIRECTOR
CONTROL TOWER

CAPTAIN

RADAR OFFICE

AMMUNITION HAND UP

AMMUNITION TRUNK

'B' 4·7 IN. GUN

'A' 4·7 IN. GUN

ARK VIII GUNS
RK VII MTG

POM POM
MAGAZINE

4·7 IN. MAGAZINE

4·7 IN. SHELL ROOM

TRANSMITTING
STATION

SUN ELEVATION
ND TRAINING

RADAR OFFICES AND AERIALS
MAY HAVE DIFFERENT POSITIONS
FROM THOSE ILLUSTRATED

BARREL

SEALING COLLAR

Q.F. 4 INCH MARK XVI* GUN

TOP SECRET

This book is for the information and guidance of Flag Officers, and of Commanding Officers of H.M. ships. The latter may, at their discretion, communicate any or all of it to their seconds-in-command, and, in large ships, to heads of departments.

Such officers are to be warned of the importance of maintaining secrecy with regard to its contents, and are to be ordered never to discuss the subject in places where their remarks may be overheard by those who are not known to have seen the book.

THE
ROYAL NAVY
OFFICER'S
POCKET-BOOK, 1944

Compiled and introduced by Brian Lavery

C
CONWAY
B L O O M S B U R Y
LONDON · NEW DELHI · NEW YORK · SYDNEY

INTRODUCTION

When Sir Alec Guinness was asked what was the best performance he had ever given, he did not mention *Kind Hearts and Coronets*, *Tinker, Tailor, Soldier, Spy* or even *Star Wars*. Instead he referred to 'That of a very inefficient, undistinguished, junior officer in the Royal Navy Volunteer Reserve.' For in May 1943, 'I was in dubious command of LCI(L) [landing craft infantry (large)] 124 with a crew of twenty.... We were all very young and inexperienced; my own lack of know-how and swift rash judgements hampered the Allied Cause like small but irritating gnatbites.'[1]

By mid-1943 the Royal Navy had endured nearly four years of total conflict, and expanded from 204,562 officers and men, including Royal Marines and reserves at the beginning of 1939, to a total of 660,000 in June 1943. It had to go well outside its normal recruitment range to find temporary officers from among those had no experience of the sea. Young men were conscripted into the Royal Navy. Possible officers were selected at a basic training camp, mostly on the basis of previous education, for the navy believed that high standards of literacy and numeracy were essential to get though the intensive course.

The selected men, known as CW candidates, were sent to sea for at least three months' active service as ordinary seamen, followed by an interview by a group of retired admirals. After that, the successful candidates were sent to HMS *King Alfred*, a shore training camp at Hove, with satellites at Lancing College and Mowden School. They were to train as 'seamen' or 'executive' officers. Engineers, aircrew and other specialists were recruited and trained separately.

King Alfred was commanded by Captain John Pelly, who had retired from the navy in 1934 and was recalled at the start of the war. He interviewed each cadet personally, but otherwise he was a rather retiring figure. His stated aim was,

> ...to instil in every man the alertness, enthusiasm, broadminded-ness, sense of responsibility, conscience and good humour (as well as a basic knowledge of technical subjects) which centuries of Service experience have shown to be necessary if a Naval Officer is to carry out his normal duties.[2]

By 1943 trainees were assumed to be 'proficient in the very elementary knowledge of seamanship, founded on the "Seaman's Pocket Book"', though not all came up to standard.[3] After around three months' training, successful candidates were commissioned as temporary officers and wore the wavy stripes of the Royal Naval Volunteer Reserve, though they were not volunteers. Those who failed the course at *King Alfred* were sent ignominiously to spend the rest of the war on the lower deck. Passes were commissioned as sub-lieutenants with a single stripe on each arm. Those over 25 were likely to be promoted to full lieutenant quite quickly. Each man was given a choice of which type of ship he wanted to serve in, but the needs of the service were paramount. Destroyers were the most glamorous, closely followed by the fast, light craft of coastal forces. The greatest number of newly trained officers went to the two areas of largest growth in the navy: landing craft that would put the troops ashore in North Africa, Italy and Normandy, and the escort vessels that would defeat the U-boats in the Battle of the Atlantic and ensure the supply chain that was essential in winning the war.

In landing craft and the small ships used by coastal forces, promotion to command of a ship was often quite fast. A newly commissioned officer might spend a few months as first lieutenant before taking charge of a landing craft with a crew of about ten, and perhaps six tanks or 200 troops on board for a landing. Escort vessels were much larger, with up to ten officers and 150 men. Most *King Alfred* graduates would take charge of a watch at sea, and take responsibility for the welfare of a division of seamen. Each would also be responsible for a part of the ship's equipment as an anti-submarine, anti-aircraft or gunnery officer, signals or radar officer, and perhaps might undertake further training for the role. A few, such as the novelist Nicholas Monsarrat, would eventually take command of escort vessels after several years of service.

THE DOCUMENTS

There is no single document that sums up the experience of naval officers during the Second World War, but the seven pamphlets reproduced here deal with almost every aspect of life, except for fighting, and technical subjects like engineering. They include seamanship, naval law, leading officers and men, battle casualties, etiquette and paperwork. Together they give a very vivid picture of life on board a warship, and the great responsibilities borne by those who commanded them. In general, the Royal Navy was some way behind the United States Navy in producing clear, readable material for trainees. Mostly it relied on out-of-date official books, designed for career officers in big ships. These pamphlets were mostly produced informally, but they already reflected a great deal of wartime experience as well as centuries of tradition. They describe the duties of naval officers and the expectations placed on them during the almost intolerable strain of a relentless war. They are printed here roughly in the order of the seniority of those they were intended for, to give a progressive view of a wartime officer's career. They start with a manual for officer training, then through the duties and etiquette of medical officers and of junior officers in HMS *Duncan*. The last three deal with the responsibilities of captains, who might be very inexperienced and quite junior in rank in wartime.

1. The Officer's Aide Memoire

Standard naval textbooks on subjects like navigation were too long to be digested easily, while there were no modern works on how to run a small ship. The *Officers Aide Memoire*, issued under Captain Pelly's name in September 1943, was intended to fill this gap. He acknowledged that the leadership section came from 'various sources'. In fact most of it is taken from the instructions issued to newly joined officers in HMS *Hood* by Captain Francis Pridham, which was in its second edition by January 1938. At first sight it seems strange that a document intended for regular officers in the biggest warship in the world should be adapted for temporary officers in landing craft, escorts, minesweepers and MTBs. But the peacetime navy did very little to train its officers in leadership. Roderick Macdonald, commissioned in 1939, wrote, 'Public school boys were for some reason assumed to have absorbed Leadership at school since it was not taught or alluded to in the training cruiser.'[4] Secondly the navy was facing a crisis with its petty officers in 1938, as many of the older men had recently retired, while the navy was going through first expansion programme for 20 years, and the strains were already showing. The *Aide Memoire* also included much detail on ship administration, and a thumbnail sketch of the principles of navigation. It had many references to paragraphs in the *King's Regulations and Admiralty Instructions*, for it was found in wartime that 'K.R. and A.I. is too comprehensive a volume and its relevant passages too difficult to find…'[5]

The *Aide Memoire* was produced after *King Alfred* had been operational for more than three years, when its training system was at its peak. It forms a remarkably concise distillation of 30 years' experience as a naval officer and was designed to enable an officer, who might be confronted with an administrative problem, to find the answer quickly by looking up the relevant reference to the governing regulation or authority. The *Aide Memoire* proved extremely popular to officers serving at sea, judging by the number of requests for copies from Commanding Officers.[6]

Most of its lessons in leadership and navigation are still valid today. *King Alfred* was one of the great successes of the war, training 22,500 naval officers.

2. Notes for Medical Officers

Notes for Medical Officers on Entry into the Royal Navy says as much about naval etiquette as is does about medicine, and this is not surprising, as most medical officers were withdrawn by the government from general practice and therefore had no seafaring experience. A peacetime naval medical officer would be given training in preventative medicine and the treatment of casualties. In wartime there was no time for that, and he might only have a few weeks of lectures in one of the naval hospitals at Chatham, Portsmouth or Plymouth. Unlike the executive officers from *King Alfred*, medical officers were likely to arrive on board ship with no more than a smattering of naval culture. The Notes were reissued in 1961, slightly expanded and reorganised but still recognisably based on the document of 1943.[7]

3. The Treatment of Battle Casualties Afloat

Notes for Medical Officers ends on a very high note: 'You are at the beginning of a new adventure and of new experiences ... This is a great privilege. Strive to be worthy of it.' *The Treatment of Battle Casualties Afloat* is a far more sombre document, describing the impotence of a surgeon while battle rages, and the horrors of a sucking chest wound. It was issued late in 1942, elaborating on an Admiralty Fleet Order of April that year which set up new standards for medical work in action. The procedure was de-centralised, with emphasis on distributing stations and first aid posts around the ship, and extreme caution in moving casualties in action.[8]

Surgeon-Lieutenant Ransome-Wallis's experiences in the destroyer Martin during the Russian convoys in 1942 reflects some of the difficulties mentioned in *The Treatment of Battle Casualties*. He went onto the quarterdeck during an action, as 'It was nearly impossible to do anything very much in the surgical sense whilst the ship was in action; there was far too much row going on to concentrate.' He was disturbed by his inability to help.

... I could not help wondering if I were falling short of what was required. If he lived, the boy with the broken back would end his days in a wheel-chair; the deeply unconscious man required brain surgery in the ordered quiet and efficiency of an operating theatre in some great teaching hospital with a team of surgeons, anaesthetists and skilled nursing staff, so different from a stretcher bed on the deck of my cabin in a lurching, heaving destroyer with all the row of gunfire, depth charges and the clanging on the hull as bombs exploded in the sea.[9]

4. HMS *Duncan* – Captain's Standing Orders

Commander Peter Gretton was already a very experienced escort officer by the time he wrote *Duncan's* standing orders in July 1943. He entered the Royal Navy as a cadet in 1926, and spent most of his time in destroyers from 1938 onwards. He became senior officer of the Seventh Escort Group in November 1942. During the spring 1943 he led the group through its greatest battles, escorting three convoys: HX 231 from Halifax to the United Kingdom; ONS 5 outward to the USA; and SC 130 back to Britain. Together they formed the turning point of the Battle of the Atlantic, and Admiral Doenitz mentioned his defeat against SC 130 when at the end of May he ordered his U-boats to withdraw from the Atlantic.

The standing orders were written during a relatively quiet period. As well as the usual problems of discipline and exhaustion in wartime crew, they reflect Gretton's determination to keep his ship up to peacetime standards.

Gretton continued to be concerned with captain's standing orders after the war. In 1961, as Flag Officer Sea Training, he was responsible for working up new ships and found that accidents were happening because some orders were 'neither clear nor comprehensive' and insisted on seeing a copy of each before it was issued.[10]

5. Your Ship

The idea of a booklet to be issued to new commanding officers of small ships first surfaced in June 1944, though the navy had already expanded to mount the D-day invasion that month. It was the idea of the new Second Sea Lord, Vice-Admiral Sir Algernon Willis. His Naval Assistant, Commander Guy Hodgkinson, chaired a meeting of experienced seamen at the Admiralty on 7 June. They quickly decided the booklet would be 'attractively set up, preferably in the form of a Commanding Officer's Pocket–book' and 'written in careful and dignified English.' It was agreed that *Your Ship* would be a good title, 'as encouraging an interested approach to the book and implying the personal relationship between the commanding Officer and his ship.' It was then decided that it should be written in three sections, entitled 'Yourself', 'Your Officers', and 'Your Men'. The members of the committee were to collate any material already available to them, and to gather more as the book was to be 'the fruits of the experience of as many commanding officers as possible.'

The committee collected several sets of orders, plus ideas from friends and acquaintances. Lieutenant A V Turner RNVR of the escort destroyer *Burwell* wrote to Captain James Tothill that he would have been 'deeply offended' if he had been given such a document when taking up his first command, but offered much advice nevertheless. It was also suggested that Pridham's document for newly-joined officers in the *Hood* might be adapted, until the Director of Naval Training pointed out that it was already being issued to new RNVR officers.

Little of this material was used and Hodgkinson largely wrote it himself. Great hopes were placed on an introduction by the Second Sea Lord, but he was a man of few words who 'despised "Public relations" believing that if a policy was right it would be seen to be so.'[11] As a result, the preface was very short. The document was ready by November and was distributed to commanding officers of all ships from destroyers downwards, including major landing craft and coastal forces, then to new commanding officers as they took up their posts.[12]

Another document, the *Aide Memoire for Small Ship Captains*, was issued in 1947 and described as an 'administrative companion' to *Your Ship*. It was four times the size, and was in fact a miscellaneous collection of advice including notes on dealing with refits in the dockyards, and in drawing up standing orders and instructions. It also incorporated much of the material which had been collected for *Your Ship* but not used.[13]

During the war Roderick Macdonald had experience of an incompetent captain (whom he nicknamed Honk) in the destroyer *Fortune*. In the 1970s he was given the chance to produce a new edition of *Your Ship*. According to his friend Admiral of the Fleet Lord Lewin, it was 'Designed to be the new Commanding Officer's guide on how to be a good Captain'. Lewin concluded, 'If only "Honk" could have read *Your Ship*.'

6. The Home Fleet Destroyer Orders

At the time when these orders were written, Irvine Glennie was Rear-Admiral (Destroyers) of the Home Fleet based in Scapa Flow. He had captained HMS *Hood* during the traumatic events during the bombardment of the French fleet at Mers-el-Kebir in 1940. He left the ill-fated ship on his promotion to rear-admiral in February 1941 and led a group of cruisers and destroyers to sink a convoy of German troops on the way to attack Crete.

Destroyers were the most flexible of warships, 'always on the go' according to an American naval observer.[14] They sank submarines, shot down aircraft, escorted battleships and aircraft carriers, and launched torpedo attacks. They took part in combined operations, rescued survivors and fought harder than any ships in the war. One hundred and fifty-four were lost, more than were in commission at the beginning of the war and more than a third of all losses of major warships. Because of the great range of their operations, they could not always rely on finding shore support and each destroyer had to learn to become self-reliant.

Regular RN officers mostly commanded destroyers, but many of them had been promoted much faster than in peacetime and were not fully experienced in seamanship and navigation. A large part of Glennie's document is devoted to avoiding elementary mistakes such as misreading the chart or hitting a jetty. He takes the opposite view from Pridham and Pelly – the expression 'safety first' is used positively. Most of his orders are only an outline, to be filled in by the officer in command with reference to King's Regulations, Admiralty Fleet Orders, official handbooks and local orders.

The section on Action Messing was clearly added later, as it refers to the sinking of the *Scharnhorst* on Boxing Day 1943. Most destroyers were fed on the antiquated Standard Ration and Messing Allowance System. Each mess appointed a cook of the day, who prepared the food and took it to the ship's galley to be cooked. Clearly this was impossible to use in a long action, when the men might be at their stations for hours at a time. Each mess tended to be jealous of its privileges and property, but Glennie's orders compelled them to share some of their food, and set up an organisation that cut across the traditional structures.

Guy Hodgkinson later collated a further document, *Notes on the Handling and Safety of Ships*, which was based closely on Glennie's orders. It was not issued generally during the war, although its inclusion of basic seamanship practice might have proved particularly useful for the young men of the RNVR. Large parts of it were later incorporated into the *Aide Memoire for Small Ship Captains* in 1947.

7. Dealing with Mutiny

By March 1944 the end of the European War was in sight and Admiral Willis began to worry about the aftermath. He noticed that 'We have seldom got through a major war without some breakdown of morale varying from serious mutiny down to vociferous expressions of dissension and dissatisfaction.' He was aware that naval mutinies had led to social breakdown in Russia and Germany at the end of the last war, and even in peacetime the Invergordon mutiny of 1931 had forced Britain off the gold standard and undermined the confidence of naval officers. Furthermore, there were likely to be specific problems if the war in the Pacific went on for years.

> ...some of the ingredients which go to make trouble of the type referred to seem likely to exist when the Germans are defeated and the full realisation that for the Navy this will mean an even greater effort in order to defeat Japan is brought home to the personnel. We shall no longer be fighting for our existence, the homeland will no longer be in danger, many of the other two services will be released to industry and at the same time personnel of the Navy, which must be kept at full strength, will be required to do more foreign service than ever.[15]

Willis wanted to make sure that all officers were 'mentally prepared' for such an eventuality, and commissioned a booklet to give guidance. It was quite alarming in places, with instructions that 'Shooting to kill should only be resorted to as a last extremity.' Admiral Horton of Western Approaches Command objected to its tone and its basic assumptions and claimed, '...no ordinary ship's company will resort to mass indiscipline unless they are labouring under grievances which a reasonable investigation will prove to be well founded.' Furthermore the pamphlet itself was dangerous.

> ...We have now serving a very large number of officers, even of Commander's rank in the Reserves, with relatively short experience of the traditional principles and methods of naval discipline and leadership. I feel strongly that the effect of these instructions in their present shape on many such officers,

and on the even less experienced officers to whom it is intended to be circulated, is likely to be very unsettling and to produce in them a state of anxiety and distrust which must invariably arouse similar reactions in their men.

The Admiralty took Horton's advice and the document was only circulated to very senior officers under a 'Top Secret' classification. In fact there was no great crisis, partly because the atom bomb ended the Pacific War before British forces were too deeply engaged. There were plenty of small mutinies in the later years of the war, mostly because, as Horton perceived, there were difficulties of leadership in individual ships. But there was no general mutiny and no need to bring the harsh provisions of the Addendendum to CB 3027 into play.

Brian Lavery is the author of *Churchill's Navy:*
The Ships, Men & Organisation, 1939–1945 (Conway, 2006)

Notes

1 *Blessings in Disguise*, pp 157-58
2 The *RNVR*, p 160
3 Adm 1/18958, *Seaman's Pocket-Book* reprinted by Conway, 2006
4 *Figurehead*, p 199
5 234/290
6 ADM 1/18952
7 ADM 234/146
8 Adm 182/110
9 *Two Red Stripes*, p 100
10 NMM GTN/5/7
11 *Figurehead*, pp 196 , 76
12 Adm 1/15676
13 234/290
14 Wellings, p 75
15 1/22967

CONTENTS

CHAPTER I
OFFICER'S AIDE MEMOIRE
HMS *King Alfred*, September 1943

This book is intended principally for the use of the young executive officer, who finds himself for the first time in a position of responsibility in service surroundings which are quite unlike anything he has encountered before. It is intended as a guide, both theoretical and practical, which will be useful until sufficient experience has been gained to make certain knowledge second nature.

The Leadership Section has been written with the idea of giving a helping hand to those who have the will to succeed and who may be groping in the dark for a lead of some sort towards the attainment of their ambition. It has been compiled from various sources which may be recognised by their authors whose help is gratefully acknowledged.

The remainder of the book contains advice and references of a more concrete nature concerning the everyday work of a Naval Officer which no amount of experience renders altogether dispensable.

J. N. PELLY,
Captain.

1: LEADERSHIP

Leadership is the one attribute which is common and necessary to all who wear the uniform of an officer in His Majesty's Forces, whatever their technical qualifications. It is also the one attribute which cannot be learnt in a classroom or from a textbook. An inexperienced officer can assimilate a reasonable amount of technical knowledge through the medium of tuition and textbooks, which can be increased by experience. That is a comparatively simple procedure by contrast with attaining the art of leadership, which rests so much with the personality of the individual concerned. Some are born great—to them the ability to lead presents no difficulty—others have greatness thrust upon them. Some of these have latent powers of leadership, and others have these powers to a limited extent only, which is a worry to them.

To develop the first essential of leadership, which is self confidence, must be a matter of practical experience, possibly painful to endure, demanding courage and the will to avoid the shadow and to come out into the light.

Never forget that the Ratings have few rights; but they definitely have got a right to good Officers.

BEARING AND EXAMPLE

Be smart and alert in your bearing, and always be meticulous about your dress.

Develop your voice and word of command.

Your demeanour should be cheerful and enthusiastic—it is your business to inspire enthusiasm and pride of ship and Service. Never appear bored or fed up, however irksome the work may be. The British have a capacity for cheerfulness in adversity. Give this a chance; it is infectious.

Never allow panic to show in your voice or manner; there is an ever-present tendency in your men to turn to an Officer for their cue in emergency.

KNOWLEDGE

Do not be too proud to study the Seamanship Manuals or other technical books; they are the teachings of many generations of experience.

Do not despise advice tendered to you by your subordinates.

On taking up a new job, keep your eyes and ears wide open and, unless and until you know something about it, your mouth shut. As leaders of fighting men it is your business to do your utmost to acquire knowledge and to impart it.

Never be afraid to ask questions. Bluff is a trait of the bad Officer.

Men quickly form a very shrewd opinion of your ability and of your capacity for just dealing. It is on this assessment that their readiness to follow your lead and to work with a will under you, mostly depends.

You cannot be just without knowledge.

FIRMNESS AND FAIRNESS

You can only acquire these through knowledge and the resulting confidence in yourself.

Be precise in your orders.

Think ahead, and thus avoid indecision and contradictory orders. Remember that many mistakes and much apparent slackness may be due to ignorance of what is required. Your job is to teach as well as to take charge, and to find fault only if necessary.

Ignorance may be the reason, and there are times when you could, and should, be kindly.

To obtain the essential grip on your men, be on the lookout for opportunities to nip slackness in the bud. These will not be rare. Use your voice on these occasions so that others may hear you, but do not scream or use sarcasm; a short, sharp, hard word is by no means excluded, but it must be justly deserved.

Remember that it is more difficult to tauten up a rope than to ease it away. Therefore, at first particularly, you must be alert and strict; but do not overdo it.

Do not deal harshly with a man solely for the sake of making an example of him. It sometimes happens that a Ship's Order or Regulation becomes temporarily unenforced. The initial fault then lies with those in authority, and it is not just, therefore, to drop heavily on one man, when there are possibly many others equally deserving punishment.

There are other ways of getting the 'buzz' passed around than by giving a heavy punishment.

The latitude permitted in summary punishment is best used in relation to the man rather than to the offence.

You must study, and know, the varying effects of punishments.

Once you have discovered a bad character you must catch him by watchfulness, and not by guile. By using guile you may be tempting him to commit a second offence, which is akin to leaving valuables lying about in order to tempt a suspected thief to steal them.

LOYALTY

Loyalty can start only from the top and grow downwards. It can be checked, or even destroyed, by lack of strength in the link just above.

Loyalty can flourish only when it acts both ways, i.e., be loyal to your inferiors as well as to your superiors. The former is often forgotten.

Do not risk giving the appearance of washing your hands of responsibility, or of giving a hint of criticism of high authority.

The 'Popularity Jack' is soon discovered by the sailor and immediately loses grip.

Do not discuss the failures of your young Petty Officers and men in the hearing of Wardroom Attendants or others of the Lower Deck. That is just as bad as admonishing a higher rating in front of his juniors.

At Defaulters do not lose an opportunity to speak in favour of a good man or of a man's good qualities. This is not only in justice to the man; it is of importance to the Captain or Commander. On the other hand, do not whiten a sepulchre.

Difficulties sometimes arise in your endeavour to support your Petty Officers. Like others, they are liable to make mistakes, and may wrongly bring up a man for punishment. Even so, it is rarely desirable to indicate publicly your displeasure.

Never judge a man if you have lost your temper.

LOYALTY TO YOUR SHIP

How well you did things in your last ship is of no consequence. You must avoid saying how you did things in your last ship.

The saying 'Different ships; different long-splices,' means, amongst other things, that there is more than one way of making a good long-splice.

SMARTNESS

A ship is either efficient, smart, clean and happy, or none of these things. They go hand in hand, or not at all.

It is no good an Officer putting the blame for inefficiency—which is very largely caused by unhappiness—on his ship's company.

The whole tone and efficiency of a ship depends on the Officers.

Most work and most activities can, and should, be performed in a businesslike manner. Slackness in falling-in, mustering or moving-off, quickly reacts on the whole spirit of the ship. Time is wasted; the hands are fallen-in earlier and the Defaulters List grows.

Points to remember before ordering your Uniform . . .

By Hector Powe

Illustrated by
Lieut. R. McLean, R.N.V.R.

WHEN you enter upon the final stages of your course you will be required to order Officer's Uniform in readiness for the time when you receive your commission.

This is not a specially easy task, most Cadet Ratings will be taxing their already weary brains with "dog-watch" studies and compulsory lectures and will find that there simply isn't time to run around collecting data from the various officially approved tailors.

It is hoped that these notes will be of assistance in telling you what to look for. Here are some points to bear in mind.

Officer's Uniform should automatically make a man look quietly well dressed. There is nothing obtrusive about it but in keeping with the tradition of the silent service, it is a silent expression of efficiency.

To achieve this, three main factors are necessary—good cloth, good craftmanship and good taste. Therefore, make sure that you deal with a house of sound repute which cannot afford to jeopardise its good reputation.

Actually, to safeguard you in this direction steps have been taken by the Naval Authorities to ensure that only officially approved tailors are permitted to serve Cadet Ratings—a step which we fully endorse.

CAPS. Remember, the Cap is most important. It can make or mar your appearance. Invest in a good one, it will repay you by keeping its shape and style throughout a long life.

We are tailors and not hatters, but we see to it that our caps are supplied only by leading houses such as Lincoln Bennet, etc. You need only state your preference.

GREY FLANNELS. You will need Grey Flannels— we supply them in the correct shade, at the special price to Officers of thirty shillings. There have been cases of overcharging — here you are safeguarded. Incidentally, your Divisional Officer will not thank you for appearing at Divisions in that old pair of dashing Check Plus-Fours which you have been so fondly cherishing, and odd indeed are the versions of grey which may sometimes be seen. They will not enhance your reputation.

PRICES.

If you have a wily eye on a personal nest egg from your official uniform allowance and intend cutting cost in all directions we may not be able to help you; our standard of service simply will not permit such debatable indiscretions.

On the other hand, there really is no reason why you should pay through the nose for your tailor's reputation. We find that the wisest plan is to provide at least three reliable grades of cloth which will fit in with most needs and most pockets. And there is the final question of speed in delivery—a point which we watch most carefully.

THERE IS A HECTOR POWE BRANCH OPPOSITE THE ESTABLISHMENT. It will take you only a moment to cross the road and obtain our price lists. You will not be bludgeoned into buying—that I promise you and I think it will be well worth your while to have a look at us and "size us up."

HECTOR POWE

NAVAL, MILITARY, R.A.F. AND CIVIL TAILOR

2 ST. AUBYNS GARDENS, HOVE

Open also on Wednesday and Saturday afternoons

Of the two seamanlike terms 'Roundly' and 'Handsomely,' the latter should be used rarely, and not as a substitute for 'Safety First.'

'Safety First' was invented to preserve the blind and ignorant amongst shore-goers. It implies delay afloat and has no place, as we depend for safety on a quick eye and rapid action.

Do your best to preserve what might be termed the minor traditions of the Service on board. Do your best to keep such things as piping and the ringing of the ship's bell up to standard, as little things like these help to spread pride of ship.

Because we are at war there is no excuse for not casting your eye over your ship for signs of slackness foreign to the Royal Navy, such as flapping ensign halyards, ropes' ends over the side, and anything that could be described as not being ship-shape.

When going rounds of inspection, bear in mind that old adage: 'Look after the corners and the rest will look after itself.' The gun may be outwardly shining; just open the breach—you may find the Bluebell tin.

WORD OF COMMAND

A great deal can be gained by making a determined effort to improve the tone and delivery of your orders. This applies equally to seamanship and to parade ground orders, although the best manner of giving each differs somewhat.

Whenever you hear a strikingly good order (some—a few—have a gift for it) study it and mimic it. Many Officers do not make themselves heard—a bad fault.

The order 'Hoist away' can be given with every bit as much life and drive as can an order on the parade ground.

Fill up your chest before giving an order. Put enthusiasm into its tone. Give it as if you meant it.

The amount of grip which can be obtained by a good word of command is remarkable.

Men cannot work at the rush to poorly given orders. The amount of strength of body and enthusiasm exerted by your men is in proportion to the grip of the person in charge and his ability to enhearten them.

PARADE SMARTNESS

As a means to an end, there are few opportunities as valuable for building up smartness of bearing as are afforded at Divisions. Officers are expected to set a high example in their bearing, manner of giving orders, marching and saluting. Do not have too many parades, but when you do have them, insist on smartness and be smart yourself.

SALUTING

A salute is not complete until it has been smartly and properly returned. A slovenly return is bad manners.

Never try to save a man a salute by turning away from him. Look at a man as he approaches you and give him a chance to do his part unhesitatingly.

Whenever a salute is made the chin should be raised.

Officers on shore should do their utmost to avoid any chance of not noticing a salute.

The foolish, shy, sloppy manner in which many Officers return salutes and sometimes endeavour to avoid them is the principal cause of slack saluting.

Remember that a sailor is proud of his Officers; and if an Officer does not do his best to uphold his position by returning marks of respect he is letting the sailor down, in addition to being bad mannered, as the sailor expects an Officer to be a gentleman.

KNOWLEDGE IN SERVING YOUR MEN

Learn their names. You must make a sustained effort in this direction should it lie within your powers.

There is nothing more irritating to a sailor than to be addressed as 'You there' or something akin to that. He likes to know that he is known by name.

Know their pay, allowances, and opportunity for advancement. Learn their circumstances, qualities and ambitions, as unobtrusively as possible, gradually gain knowledge of their budgets and family situation, but beware of prying into a man's family affairs in a manner which might strike him as being that of a busybody.

After all is said and done, an Officer's bearing towards his men should be that of a friend, and, as a friend, a man should realise that if he is faced with professional or domestic problems that need advice, he can go to his Officers without fear to obtain it.

Learn what your men's interests are outside the Service, and their topics of conversation and discussion.

Make yourself familiar with the work of the Family Welfare Section and the Royal Navy Benevolent Trust.

Should a man come to you for advice, do not let the matter drop and be forgotten. It may well be that a subsequent enquiry as to how things are going on will sometimes bring to light that a man is still in need of further help but is averse to coming along a second time

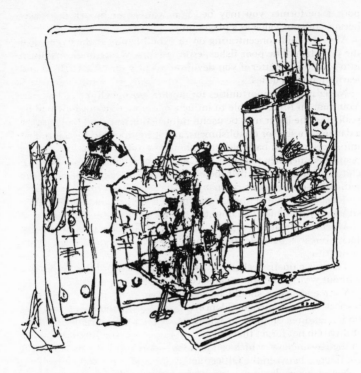

because he thinks he has already made enough fuss about it. In this connection, how many times is this heard at the Defaulter's Table? 'I put in a request but heard no more about it.' This is just cause of complaint on the part of the rating.

Do not be discouraged because a man prefers to see a more Senior Officer about his affairs. A man will often open up to you later after he has unburdened himself to an older Officer.

Study the conditions in which your men live in their ship or station, details of the serving of their food, where they write their letters, the true extent of the facilities, or lack of them, for washing, shaving and keeping their kit tidy.

Discover their recreations. We all know the experts at games; but there are dozens of others who get as much enjoyment out of a game of football as does a member of the team.

Do not be afraid to accept an invitation to play games, however poor a performer you may be. You would not be asked to play because of your value as a player only.

Always avoid concentrating on the good hands at the expense of the poor fish. The poor fishes, especially the young ones, may turn into something better if you devote some of your time to them and learn their difficulties.

Never neglect opportunities for getting into touch with a bad hat. You may, in time, be able to influence him or find out how bad he really is. The latter may be useful information one day. Bad hats are a danger in a ship or establishment, and it is important therefore that information about bad characters should be as full as possible. In this respect, remember that bad hats in a ship usually form their own cliques, as they realise that their way of life is not appreciated by the remainder of the ship's company. It should be easy to observe these cliques, and whether they are being a danger to the youngsters, a situation with which you ought to be able to deal.

Much of the above savours of the 'Paul Pry' or the 'Popularity Jack,' but it is possible to obtain this knowledge without deserving either title.

There is a quality called tact, a very misused word in many ways, without which no Officer can succeed.

Your endeavour should be to inspire in your men a feeling of respect for you and confidence in your sympathetic interest and understanding of their problems as well as in your professional ability. Do not forget that this is the basis of our treasured discipline in the Royal Navy, which can be summed up as the fruits of mutual confidence between the Officer and man.

Never turn down an application on compassionate grounds because you think it is impossible for the Captain to grant it. Through his greater experience the Captain is better able to judge and explain. Moreover, it is important that the men should realise the availability of their Captain.

It is within the competence of any Officer to show consideration to his men. Uncertainty as to whether they will be required during working hours; a sudden alteration or curtailment of a meal hour, should be avoided if possible. If it is not, pass the word as long beforehand as you can, and, if possible, give the reason. Do not forget that a man will always work better if he knows what he is working for, and if it is a question of working at what might be described as an unusual time or for an unusual time, the reason should be stated.

Never keep a boat waiting. This is as bad as keeping hands fallen-in waiting. An Officer's job is to be first on the spot, and this applies in particular to junior Officers.

Always remember that if it is ever necessary to alter the routine time for a meal the galley should be warned in plenty of time.

Always give as much information as you can about long leave dates, week-ends, and, for that matter, drafting, if possible.

The more you can interest your ship's company in what is going on the better. Moreover, you will then short-circuit the disgruntled man who spreads the yarn that they are being bully-ragged and driven unnecessarily.

It is also your business to instruct and educate your men with a view to inducing ambition to better their positions in the Service, as distinct from their rate of pay.

Many men are grateful for having their minds made up for them, and have a child-like faith in the advice of an officer they know and respect.

ENCOURAGEMENT OF YOUR
HIGHER RATINGS

There was a day when the Warrant Officer was described as the link between the Wardroom and the Lower Deck. In those days a Warrant Officer, in addition to his specialist duties, was a store-keeping officer, and, as such, the importance of his department carried much more weight than it does in these days of general messing and central store-keeping. In consequence, the modern Warrant Officer, by reason of his status as a Junior Officer who, apart from his specialist duties, plays a much larger part in the internal economy of the ship, has handed over the title 'link' to the higher rating. It is therefore of the utmost importance that you should bear in mind that the responsibilities of the higher rating are more important now than they have ever been. They should be made to feel that they are in your confidence, and they should be made to feel that they really are the men that matter. Bring them into any discussion on a job of work, drill, improvement or amenity. Not nearly enough is done by Officers to recognise the status of Higher Ratings.

Make a point of sending a word of commendation through your higher ratings, and you can follow this up later, should you so desire, by giving it in person.

On the other hand, do not expect too much of your higher ratings. You cannot expect their standard to be a very level one, as large numbers are at present being made and many are of very limited experience.

Endeavour to avoid putting a higher rating in charge of a job without first discovering whether he knows how to set about it.

Avoid showing preference to a higher rating of higher quality at the expense of the remainder. The latter, besides being far more numerous, are in more need of your assistance, and this type includes a large number who, with a little guidance, quickly grow to take a jealous pride in their work.

You must also bear in mind that the young higher ratings, and particularly the Leading Seamen, have a difficult job. They find themselves in charge of men older than themselves, some of whom endeavour to trip them up. If you spot any sign of insolence of disobedience, do not wait for the Petty Officer to complain or run the man in.

Give the higher rating the benefit of your greater knowledge by making opportunities for discussion, and, if possible, instruction. However busy you are, these opportunities will occur, possibly when you are on watch at night or closed up at your action stations.

FIGHTING QUALITIES

Endeavour to bring out the fighting qualities of your men. This should be your constant consideration, as in your position as a leader it is your business to inspire enthusiasm.

It is no easy matter to bring into proper significance the bearing that fitness has on fighting ability, which is our sole purpose and great responsibility. We are inclined to forget that even in these highly mechanised days superiority in battle is far more a matter of fighting qualities in ourselves and our men, than the calibre of guns and thickness of armour.

FORETHOUGHT

Life at sea differs essentially from life ashore. We are far more dependent at sea on the whims of the elements. These have an uncomfortable habit of upsetting our plans and routines unexpectedly unless we use forethought.

Look ahead; do not wait until something goes wrong. If you anticipate that you may run into bad weather, have that rope, that jigger, that heaving line, that strop or that hand pike handy in the place where you may want it.

Look above the level of your head, and train the men to do the same. Most of us are born with a tendency to look only along the level of our noses. Trouble usually comes from overhead, and in these days in more ways than one.

Napoleon's reply to a 'Yes Man' is well worthy of remembrance, and this is it: 'If I always appear prepared, it is because before entering on any undertaking I have meditated long and have foreseen what may occur. It is not genius which reveals to me what I should do; it is thought and meditation.' Napoleon's secret was little more than careful concentration of his thoughts, the carrying out of a mental 'dummy-run' whenever possible.

Finally, it is not possible to write a handbook on how to be an Officer and a leader. We have each to find out for ourselves the best use we can make of those particular qualities possessed by each of us in varying degrees.

2: HINTS TO AN O.O.W.
ON DEFAULTERS
O.O.W.—INVESTIGATIONS

Discipline. Good discipline in H.M. Ships is achieved primarily by the leadership of the Officers. This involves the exercise of conscious and deliberate loyalty to your Captain and Senior Officers, as well as to your subordinates, and conscious effort to make your ship efficient by your enthusiasm and hard work.

Punishments, under the King's Regulations and Admiralty Instructions (K.R. & A.I.) and the Naval Discipline Act (N.D.A.), should be used as a last resort. Bear this in mind and do your best to prevent serious cases arising.

Investigations. As Officer of the Watch (O.O.W.) all cases for investigation must be brought before you. (K.R. & A.I. Art. 537).

The following are the principal points the O.O.W. should bear in mind when carrying out an investigation:—

(1) Always see that a defaulter is ordered to 'Off Caps' before you attempt to proceed.

(2) Never allow a rating to commit himself to a further and possibly more serious offence. Therefore always stand well back from him when investigating the case.

(3) The accused must be considered innocent until you have heard the case for the prosecution and all that he may have to say in his defence, together with the evidence of any witnesses that may be called on both sides. Although it is within the discretion of the Officer of the Watch to dismiss a case, and he has (if authorised by the Captain) the power to award one day's No.16 punishment, it is preferable for an inexperienced Officer to pass on all cases to the Executive Officer.

(4) See that all witnesses are kept apart, and never allow a witness to hear what other witnesses are saying when giving evidence.

(5) Never allow yourself to become identified with the prosecution, but reserve your opinion until after you have heard both sides.

(6) Maintain a dignified calm and never express your feelings forcibly to the accused or any witness during an investigation.

(7) Bear in mind and apply, as the circumstances may require, the 'intentions' of the accused, and the 'Reasonable Man test'—e.g. What should reasonably have been expected of a man of similar rating and experience to the accused in like circumstances.

(8) Always obtain corroborative evidence of any statements made, when such evidence is available.

(9) Ascertain the truth by finding out the facts, and so form as complete a mental picture as possible of what actually took place, and never jump to conclusions.

After hearing the case, if you place the accused in the Executive Officer's Report, it is your duty to see that the charge (or charges) is correctly framed in accordance with the 'Instructions for Framing Charges' in the 'Admiralty Memo. On C.M. Procedure,' pages 78 to 88, Sections 2 to 45. This cannot be too carefully dealt with. A badly worded charge may cause considerable trouble at a later stage.

You will be responsible for presenting the case to the Executive Officer, and must therefore remember the salient features which came to light as the result of your investigations.

Warning to Accused. (K.R. & A.I., Art 537)

If, after hearing the case for the prosecution, you decide that it is so serious that it might form the subject of a Court Martial, then you must 'warn' the Accused, using the following form:—

'You are not obliged to say anything unless you wish to do so, but whatever you say will be taken down in writing and may be given in evidence. Do you quite understand?'

It would be proper for the O.O.W. to administer the 'Warning' and/or place an offender under arrest in the following cases, if such action is warranted by the facts.

Mutiny or Mutinous Conduct.

Acts of gross Indecency.

Gross Insubordination.

Striking or attempting to Strike.

Smuggling.

Theft. Any case in which a Chief or Petty Officer is accused.

Note.—This is by no means a comprehensive list, and the O.O.W. must decide when to apply this procedure to other cases. It is better to err on the side of giving the 'Warning.' It must be remembered that an admission of guilt by the accused will not be admissible in evidence at a subsequent trial unless this warning is duly given and recorded. The accused should be asked to read the written note of his statement and to sign it if he is satisfied with it.

Arrest. (Art. 507, K.R. & A.I.)

Arrest is not a punishment. It is a means to ensure the safe custody of an offender until he can be dealt with adequately. It may also, in certain circumstances, be a preventive measure—e.g., a man guilty of gross insubordination or mutiny would be placed under 'close arrest' to prevent his example or influence affecting the Ship's Company.

Should the O.O.W. place a man under arrest he must at once inform the Commanding Officer that he has done so.

Drunkenness. (Art. 462a K.R.)

The O.O.W. is responsible for deciding whether a man is drunk or not. His decision must be based on the following criterion:—

Is the man fit in all respects to carry out his duty? (And that means any duty which a man of his Rate could legitimately be called upon to perform).

If, in the opinion of the O.O.W., the answer to this question is no, and providing that the man's condition is due to the intoxicating effect of liquor, then the man is drunk.

If yes, then he is sober.

Note.—There is no such thing in Naval Law as 'Having Drink taken.' A man is either Drunk or Sober.

Before interviewing an apparently drunken or excited man, the O.O.W. should have adequate force (Escort) immediately available. When possible, the escort should not be seen by the accused, but be in a position to take immediate action if and when considered necessary.

Sentry's Charge. A drunken man must be placed under a Sentry's charge. (This must not be confused with arrest). It is done solely in the man's own interests in order to ensure his safety and to prevent his having opportunity of committing himself further. It must not, and should never be considered in any sense, as a form of punishment.

If the offender is a Chief or Petty Officer, it is customary to place him in the care of the President of his Mess, but obviously this will not apply if he is at all violent or obstreperous; he must then be placed under the Sentry's charge.

When the O.O.W. has placed a man under the Sentry's charge, he must at once report the action he has taken to the C.O.

Medical Attention. The O.O.W. must have the man examined by a Medical Officer if he is seen to be suffering from some physical injury, or is insensible, of if the Officer of the Watch is not entirely satisfied that his condition is due to drink. This is necessary because illnesses have occasionally been mistaken for drunkenness.

In this connection, the following is an extract from Section 462a of the N.D.A.

'The responsibility for deciding in the first instance in cases of alleged drunkenness whether an officer or man is in a fit state to perform his duties, rests with the Commanding Officer; but in a case of this nature, should there be any doubt as to the reason of the accused's condition, it is desirable that the opinion of the Medical Officer should be obtained at once. Otherwise a plea of sickness may be brought forward at the court-martial or other later investigation, and the omission of this precaution may be taken advantage of by the accused, with the result that a guilty person may escape the punishment due to his offence.'

For further information on the subject of drunkenness and drinking to excess see Notes 1 and 2 in Section 462a of the N.D.A.

Insubordination. (Sec. 17, N.D.A.).

(*a*) **Disobedience**. In cases of alleged disobedience, a detailed examination of the *facts* is especially necessary. Carry out the investigation on some such lines as these:—

(1) Was it a direct order or a message?
(2) Was it properly heard?
(3) Was it properly understood?
(4) Was it deliberately disobeyed?
(5) Was it repeated?

And, from another aspect (though you should be careful not to criticize the person who gave the order, whilst the accused is present)

(6) Was it a 'reasonable' order, and given with due regard to the circumstances?

Though negative answers to any of the above questions may not excuse the offence of disobedience, they may very well affect the degree of guilt.

A man guilty of wilful disobedience to a direct order from his Superior Officer should normally be placed under arrest. 'Did wilfully disobey the lawful command of . . . .' (*Vide* Instructions for Framing Charges) 'when ordered to . . . .'

Standing Orders (e.g. Ship's Orders or Regulations).

Cases of contravention of a general order as opposed to a specific order are not classed a insubordination but are charged under Sec. 43, N.D.A.—'Was guilty of an act to the Prejudice of good order and Naval Discipline.' This is not so serious in itself but is dependent upon the subject matter of the charge, and, for example, becomes very serious if it is a case of Smuggling or deliberate evasion of the Censorship Regulations.

(*b*) **Using Threatening Language, Etc.**

All cases of 'Using threatening or insulting language' to, or of 'behaving with contempt towards' a superior Officer, are charged under Section 17 N.D.A. There is no absolute criterion by which to judge the seriousness of the case; each must be considered on its merits.

Striking. (Sec. 16 N.D.A.)

To constitute a charge of striking, or attempting to strike, the offence must be against the accused's Superior Officer, whether or not such Superior Officer was in execution of his office.

A 'Warning' (K.R. & A.I., Art. 537) should always be given in such cases and it will generally be desirable to place the man under arrest.

Medical Evidence. Where possible Medical evidence should be obtained at the preliminary investigation. (Art. 46a (ii), K.R. & A.I.).

Definition of Superior Officer. (See Notes under Section 16 N.D.A.) Any Officer, Petty Officer or non-commissioned Officer senior to the accused.

Note.—Leading Seamen are not Superior Officers within the meaning of this Act. Insubordination or Striking offences against Leading Seamen are dealt with under Section 43 N.D.A.).

'An act to the prejudice of good order and Naval discipline.'

Quarrelling or Fighting. (Section 18 N.D.A.)

May or may not be serious, depending upon the circumstances.

Theft. (Sec. 45 N.D.A.)

An accusation of this nature should be charged as an ordinary law offence under Sec. 45 N.D.A. Comprehensive instructions are given in the Admiralty Memorandum (pages 84-88), which should be carefully studied. It is regarded as a serious offence.

Note.—Charges of being in possession of articles of clothing, etc., belonging to another rating are generally not dealt with as 'theft' (which may be difficult to prove) but as 'not handing over to the proper authority (here specify the articles and their owners) which to his knowledge had come into his possession without the consent of the owners.'

Power of Search. The O.O.W. has power to order a search of a man's kit and effects. This derives from the Authority of the Captain whose direct representative he is. The search is carried out in the presence of an Officer, by the M.A.A., Coxswain, or their deputies, if possible, in the presence of the accused.

Indecent Offences. It is essential in any charges of indecent conduct that—

  (*a*) The investigation shall be made at once no matter at what time it occurs;

  (*b*) that all persons implicated should be 'warned.';

  (*c*) that medical examination shall be made forthwith;

  (*d*) that evidence shall be taken down in writing and signed.

If these things are not done at once it is almost impossible to get the necessary evidence afterwards.

Note.—For further details concerning 'Indecent Offences' see C.A.F.O. 648/40.

References. Officers are recommended to study Chapter XII, K.R. & A.I. and Admiralty Memorandum on Naval C.M. Procedure, with special reference to these instructions for Framing Charges (pages 78-88) and Appendix VIII, 'Rules of Evidence.' If these are not available on board they should be studied at the Base.

Experience. Take every opportunity of attending Captain's and Commander's Defaulters whether or not you are concerned with the cases being dealt with.

See K.R. and A.I. App. XVII for details of full pay, progressive pay, allowances and qualifications for Sub. And Non-Sub. Ratings.

For details of war time advancements, see A.F.O's.

Permanent advancement; only C.S. and S.S. eligible, and must pass E.T. part I, serve 12 months in seagoing ship, and serve the prescribed period of V.G. conduct. Date for commencement of V.G. conduct time is noted on Conduct Sheet.

A man disrated for misconduct is re-advanced to 'temporary' rating, awaiting his turn on Depot Roster for 'permanent' rating.

For H.O. ratings, Reservists, Pensioners, R.F.R., time expired men and R.N.V.R., advancement to L.Sea. and above is temporary, no E.T. required, and period of seagoing service is 6 months.

See A.F.O. 864/42 for use of Form S.507 (described in K.R. and A.I. Appendix XXII p. 286). See also amendments to A.F.Os.

RATING	QUALIFICATIONS REQUIRED	REMARKS		
Boy to Ord. Sea.	Age 18 (or 17½ if Boy has passed E.T. part II). Must pass Seamanship exam. for A.B. Specially recommended by Commanding Officer.	All advancement up to A.B. is Permanent		
Ord. Sea. to A.B.	C.S. and S.S. (ex Boys), 9 months or 6 months / H.O. and S.S., 12 months or 9 months — With minimum of 4 months' sea service / Must pass in Sea., G. and T for A.B.	If unable to pass these examinations for reasons out of man's control, he may be advanced Acting A.B. and confirmed when qualified		
		MINIMUM PERIOD OF V.G. CONDUCT REQUIRED		
		Temporary	Permanent	Re-advancement
A.B. to L. Sea.	Can pass professionally at any time after rating A.B. Advancement is "Acting" for 12 months from date of seeing Captain to be rated.	6 months	12 months	6 months K.R. and A.I. 560
L.Sea. to P.O.	Can pass at any time after rating L.Sea. Advancement is Acting; as for L. Sea.	6 months	18 months	6 months
P.O. to C.P.O.	Must serve minimum period of 3 years after passing for P.O. and five years' combined service as Ldg. Sea. and P.O. Recommended on S.507	3 months	3 years	2 years

See A.F.O. 6376/42 for all temporary advancement to L.Sea., P.O. and C.P.O.

Form B, 13 from Depot to Captain for all permanent advancements, General Service, Patrol Service and Boom Defence.

3: ESSENTIAL REFERENCES

Good Conduct Badges.
Qualifications for Award—K.R. and A.I. Chapter XII Section III.
Restoration of G.C.B.—K.R. and A.I. Article 564 (3).

Good Conduct Medal.
Qualifications for Award—K.R. and A.I. Chapter XII Section IVI

Requests. See K.R. and A.I. Article 9. **Complaints.** See Article 10.

Welfare. (*a*) There are Family Welfare Officers at each main Depot to give advice on domestic problems.

(*b*) The Royal Naval Benevolent Trust has representatives in the Fleet and at most Bases. The Trust is for the purpose of relieving any authentic cases of distress that may affect directly or indirectly any Rating or his dependents.

(*c*) The War Service Grants Advisory Committee recommends additional allowances when calling-up has resulted in a serious drop in income. Application forms can be obtained at most Post Offices, or at Pay Offices.

Service Certificate. (S. 459): Character and Efficiency assessed on p. 4 of S. 459 yearly on 31st December, also on day preceding 18th birthday, and on final discharge from Service, or on desertion. See K.R. and A.I., 605, 607. Kit List, S. 98. Divisional Record Sheet, S.264 (confidential). History sheet.

Duties of Divisional Officer. See K.R. and A.I. Chapter XXXII, 1158a. See also articles 9 (4), 514 (8) and 514a (4).

507	Arrest.	538	(1) and 577 (5) and Court Martial memoranda pp. 75-85 wording of charges.
509	Logging Offences.		
514	Duties and Privileges of Petty Officers.		
514a	Duties and Privileges of Leading Ratings.	536	(3) Daily Record, and Punishment Returns.
518	Naval Custody.	520a	Articles found lying about
540	Tables I and II, Normal Maximum summary punishments.	535	Power to award Punishment.
		536	Delegated Authority.
578	Scale of mulcts for Leave breaking.	537	Investigation of complaints, etc.
		539	Special directions.

Discipline. K.R. and A.I. Chapter XII.
K.R. and A.I. Affecting All Officers.

Observance and enforcement, Article 1. Conduct, Articles 6 and 7.

Attendance on Board, Applications for Leave, Movements on Leave, etc.: Articles 4, 513, 639, 640 and 643.

Responsibility of Officers signing accounts and books. Articles 33 and 35.

Responsibility of C.O. A.F.O. 2832/42.

Order of Rank and Command: Article 172. Authority of O.O.W.: Article 178.

Miscellaneous: Mails, Articles 1095-1099. Meal Hours, Articles 627, 628.

Note:—Much of this information is liable to alteration from time to time, and care should be taken to keep this section up-to-date from the latest A.F.O.'s, Amendments to K.R. and A.I., etc.

4: SHIP'S BUSINESS

Messing. Ships are now messed under the following systems:—
(*a*) General Mess.
(*b*) Modified General Mess.
(*c*) Victualling Allowance (Small Ships).

Victualling Allowance.
Allowance 1s. 10d. per day, per man, noon to noon.
Forms—

Victualling and Check Books	S.257, S.257b.
Mess Book	S.1057.
Quarterly Provision Account	S.1061.
Abstract of Soap and Tobacco Issued	S.78.

Abstract of Clothing Issue Notes	S.1048.
Mess Chit Book	S.77.
Losses of Victualling Stores	S.1251.
Soap and Tobacco Issue Note	S.1047.
Clothing Issue Note	S.80.

Rum. See K.R. and A.I. 1824-1834. Neat rum to Chief and P.O.s only; mixed with 2 parts water for remainder.

Daily Issue Book	S.71a	1 jar = 8 pints = 64 tots.
Spirit Issue Book	S.1059	1 tot = 1/8 pint.
Spirit Stoppage Book	S.76B	Rum is NOT duty free stores.

Naval Stores. Manual of Naval Storekeeping. B.R.4. Rate Book, O.U. 5409/43, etc., and A.F.O.'s for Small Ships.

Casual Demands and Demand for Permanent Stores on Naval Dockyard	S.134d
Demand on Naval Stores in base or ship	S.156
General utility transfer note between ships	S.549
Survey note for returning stores to Dockyard	S.331
Note for returning stores to base or parent ship	S.1091
Periodic Demand for consumable stores	S.1094
Naval Stores lost by accident	S.1096
Naval Stores lost by neglect	S.126
Inventory, Permanent Loan, inside	S.1099

Inventory, small craft:

| Permanent Stores | F.A.21 | Consumable Stores | F.A.23 |

Gangway Forms and Books.

Gangway Wine and Spirit Book: All details concerning duty free goods (wines, spirits, beer and tobacco, including cigars and cigarettes) are entered in this book when brought on board or taken out of the ship.

Short Leave Book: Names of all ratings proceeding on short leave are entered therein, those on long leave are 'checked' to leave.

Registered Letter Book: Contains record of all registered letters and parcels received, signed by recipient.

Non-Public Funds.

K.R. and A.I. 630 Administration of Canteens and funds.
1138 Officers messes and accounts.
1105 para 4 Public and non-public cash.
635 Subsidiary and non-public funds.
1138a Miscellaneous funds.
1105 para 11 and 12 Non-public funds on paying off.
A.F.O.s 2897/40 Disposal of funds.

Abbreviated Titles of Authorities, as used in signals, etc.
Base:
F.O.I.C. Flag Officer in Charge.   P.W.S.S. Port War Signal Station.
N.O.I.C. Naval Officer in Charge.   K.B.O. Kite Balloon Officer.

R.N.O. Resident Naval Officer.
L.N.O. Local Naval Officer.
X.D.O. Extended Defence Officer.
C.X.O. Chief Examination Officer.
K.H.M. King's Harbour Master.
N.C.S.O. Naval Control Service Officer.

R.O. Routeing Officer.
S.O.(I) Staff Officer, Intelligence.
S.O.O. Staff Officer, Operations.
B.A.O. Base Accountant Officer.
B.E.O. Base Engineering Officer.
N.S.O. Naval Store Officer.

Dockyard.

A.S.	Admiral Superintendent.
C.D. and D.S.	Captain of Dockyard and Deputy Superintendent. Berthing ships, Seamanship dept. of the Dkyd. Boats, rigging, cables, boatswain's stores, etc.
M.C.D.	Manager, Constructor's Department. All building work, repairs and alterations to ships.
M.E.D.	Manager, Engineering Dept. All Engine Room Gun Mountings and tubes.
S.C.E.	Superintending Civil Engineer. Buildings, and roads on shore.
S.E.E.	Superintending Electrical Engineer. All electrical work.
S.N.S.O.	Superintending Naval Store Officer. Naval Stores and oil fuel.
S.A.S.O.	Superintending Armament Supply Officer. Naval Ordnance Stores.
F.O.G.O.	Fitting out Gunnery Officer.
F.O.G.M.O.	Fitting out Gun Mountings Officer.
V.S.O.	Victualling Store Officer.

Miscellaneous.

A. and A's.: Alterations and Additions. See K.R. and A.I. Article 710.

Defect Lists. Pink Defect Lists comprise items affecting the fighting and seagoing efficiency of the ship.

White Defect Lists are made out for all other defects, see Article 707.

Supplementary Defect Lists cover defects arising after Defect Lists have been submitted.

Covering Power of Paint: 1 cwt.=3,000 sq. ft. 1 gall.=50 sq. yds.

Note:—Much of this information is liable to alteration from time to time, and care should be taken to keep this section up-to-date from the latest A.F.O.'s, Amendments to K.R. and A.I., etc.

5: NAVIGATIONAL AIDE MEMOIRE
CORRECTION OF COURSES AND BEARINGS
The Slewing Method.

(*a*) **To Lay Off a Compass Course (or Bearing).**

1. Straddle the Magnetic Rose with the ruler on the course (or bearing).
2. Look up the Deviation for the Ship's Head; combine this with the *change* of variation from the chart to give a total correction E. or W.
3. Slew the '*North End*' of the ruler the amount and direction of this total correction.
4. Centre the ruler across the rose and then move off.

(*b*) **To Convert a True Course to Compass Course.**

1. Read off the Course on the Magnetic rose, and look up the Deviation for this Course.
2. Slew the '*South End*' of the ruler, the amount and direction of the Deviation (combined with any change of variation).
3. Centre the ruler and read off the Compass Course on the Magnetic rose.

(*c*) **To obtain the Deviation from a Transit.**
1. Move the ruler across from the transit on the chart to straddle the magnetic rose.
2. The amount and direction that you would have to move the '*South End*' of the ruler to give the compass bewaring of the transit is the Deviation (after making allowance for change of variation, if any).

(*For alternative method see Ad. Man. Navigation, Vol. I* (1938), *p.*14).

TIDAL STREAM TRIANGLES
'When you know the course to steer, straightway plot your D.R. clear, but, if asked to find the course, lay your *tide set* off at source.'

1. **Find Course made good, and S.M.G.**
Use any convenient time interval. Lay off the course and distance through the water. From the 2nd D.R. lay off the *drift*, to give T, the 'E.P.'
FT gives course and distance made good. It is the **ship's track** and may be referred to as such.
S.M.G. is then readily deduced.

2. **Find Course to steer to make good a given Course.**

Use an hourly triangle. Plot the 'Course to be made good.' Lay off the *drift* FG; then from G 'cut in' with *available speed* to obtain Course to steer. FE gives the S.M.G.

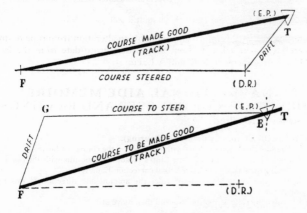

INTERCEPTING (THE ENEMY)

Basic Principle. The (enemy) ship may be out of sight, but if the true bearing remains constant then collision (interception) must occur.

1. Plot on estd. posn. of Enemy and Own Ship *to the time when your Course will be altered.*

2. Plot *on* estd. run of E in 1 hour (E A).

3. Transfer true bearing line to pass through A.

4. From O, 'cut in' with own available speed (OB). OB is the Course to steer.

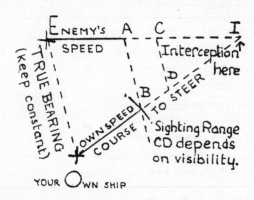

The same method can be used to arrive at any position relative to the enemy, by using the true bearing of the relative position. Simply, a fictitious ship in that position has to be intercepted.

USE OF SUNRISE/SET AND MOONRISE/SET TABLES

EX.—Find Z.T. of Sunset on 1st May, 1943, in 51° N, 39° W.

L.M.T. Sunset	19	20	1st May (From Nautical Almanac)
Long	02	36W	(W plus, E minus).

G.M.T.	21	56	1st May	NOTE—
Zone	3			B.S.T. is the time of Zone—1
				M.S.T. ,, ,, Zone—2

Z.T.	18	56	(+3) 1st May.

Similar work using MOONRISE/SET Tables will give an approximate result.

NAUTICAL TWILIGHT problems (required for operational purposes) are worked as for the SUN, from the appropriate Tables.

SPEED-DISTANCE TABLE

TIME RUN IN MINUTES

Knots	10	20	30	40	50	60	1	2	3	4	5	6	7	8	9
10	1.7	3.3	5.0	6.7	8.3	10.0	.2	.3	.5	.7	.8	1.0	1.2	1.3	1.5
11	1.8	3.7	5.5	7.3	9.2	11.0	.2	.4	.6	.7	.9	1.1	1.3	1.5	1.7
12	2.0	4.0	6.0	8.0	10.0	12.0	.2	.4	.6	.8	1.0	1.2	1.4	1.6	1.8
13	2.2	4.3	6.5	8.7	10.8	13.0	.2	.4	.7	.9	1.1	1.3	1.5	1.7	2.0
14	2.3	4.7	7.0	9.3	11.7	14.0	.2	.5	.7	.9	1.2	1.4	1.6	1.9	2.1
15	2.5	5.0	7.5	10.0	12.5	15.0	.3	.5	.8	1.0	1.3	1.5	1.7	2.0	2.3
16	2.7	5.3	8.0	10.7	13.3	16.0	.3	.5	.8	1.1	1.3	1.6	1.9	2.1	2.4
17	2.8	5.7	8.5	11.3	14.2	17.0	.3	.6	.9	1.1	1.4	1.7	2.0	2.3	2.6
18	3.0	6.0	9.0	12.0	15.0	18.0	.3	.6	.9	1.2	1.5	1.8	2.1	2.4	2.7
19	3.2	6.3	9.5	12.7	15.8	19.0	.3	.6	1.0	1.3	1.6	1.9	2.2	2.5	2.9
20	3.3	6.7	10.0	13.3	16.7	20.0	.3	.7	1.0	1.3	1.7	2.0	2.3	2.7	3.0
21	3.5	7.0	10.5	14.0	17.5	21.0	.4	.7	1.1	1.4	1.8	2.1	2.5	2.8	3.1
22	3.7	7.3	11.0	14.7	18.3	22.0	.4	.7	1.1	1.5	1.8	2.2	2.6	2.9	3.3
23	3.8	7.7	11.5	15.3	19.2	23.0	.4	.8	1.2	1.5	1.9	2.3	2.7	3.1	3.4
24	4.0	8.0	12.0	16.0	20.0	24.0	.4	.8	1.2	1.6	2.0	2.4	2.8	3.2	3.6
25	4.2	8.3	12.5	16.7	20.8	25.0	.4	.8	1.3	1.7	2.1	2.5	2.9	3.3	3.7
26	4.3	8.7	13.0	17.3	21.7	26.0	.4	.9	1.3	1.7	2.2	2.6	3.0	3.5	3.9
27	4.5	9.0	13.5	18.0	22.5	27.0	.5	.9	1.4	1.8	2.3	2.7	3.2	3.6	4.0
28	4.7	9.3	14.0	18.7	23.3	28.0	.5	.9	1.4	1.9	2.3	2.8	3.3	3.7	4.2
29	4.8	9.7	14.5	19.3	24.2	29.0	.5	1.0	1.5	1.9	2.4	2.9	3.4	3.9	4.4
30	5.0	10.0	15.0	20.0	25.0	30.0	.5	1.0	1.5	2.0	2.5	3.0	3.5	4.0	4.5
31	5.2	10.3	15.5	20.7	25.8	31.0	.5	1.0	1.6	2.1	2.6	3.1	3.6	4.1	4.7
32	5.3	10.7	16.0	21.3	26.7	32.0	.5	1.1	1.6	2.1	2.7	3.2	3.7	4.3	4.8
33	5.5	11.0	16.5	22.0	27.5	33.0	.6	1.1	1.7	2.2	2.8	3.3	3.9	4.4	5.0
34	5.7	11.3	17.0	22.7	28.3	34.0	.6	1.1	1.7	2.3	2.8	3.4	4.0	4.5	5.1
35	5.8	11.7	17.5	23.3	29.2	35.0	.6	1.2	1.8	2.3	2.9	3.5	4.1	4.7	5.3
36	6.0	12.0	18.0	24.0	30.0	36.0	.6	1.2	1.8	2.4	3.0	3.6	4.2	4.8	5.4
37	6.2	12.3	18.5	24.7	30.8	37.0	.6	1.2	1.9	2.5	3.1	3.7	4.3	4.9	5.6
38	6.3	12.7	19.0	25.3	31.7	38.0	.6	1.3	1.9	2.5	3.2	3.8	4.4	5.1	5.7
39	6.5	13.0	19.5	26.0	32.5	39.0	.7	1.3	2.0	2.6	3.3	3.9	4.6	5.2	5.9
40	6.7	13.3	20.0	26.7	33.3	40.0	.7	1.3	2.0	2.7	3.3	4.0	4.7	5.3	6.0

TABLE GIVES DISTANCE IN MILES

Whenever possible use the new Slide Rule (A.F.O. 3297'43)

A GUIDE TO WORKING A SUNSIGHT

Z.T.	Zone Time, and date.
Z.	West +, East — ; (B.S.T. = — 1 M.S.T. = — 2).
G.D.	Greenwich Date. (Make G.M.T. agree with G.D.)
D.W.T.	Deck Watch Time.
Error	plus if slow; minus if fast.
G.M.T.	Greenwich Mean time, and date.
E.	for G.M.T. Always plus.
G.H.A.	Greenwich Hour Angle True Sun.
Long.	Plus if east: minus if west. (1°=4 mins. of time).
L.H.A.	(i) Local Hour Angle True Sun.
Lat.	(ii) Latitude of E.P. or D.R. Position.
Dec.	(iii) Declination for G.M.T.
~	(iv) For same names subtract (ii) and (iii)
	For opposite names add (ii) and (iii)
	(v) Log haversine (i)
	(vi) Log cosine (ii)
	(vii) Log cosine (iii)
	(viii) Sum of (v), (vi) and (vii)
	(ix) natural haversine (viii)
	(x) natural haversine (iv)
	(xi) Sum of (ix) and (x)
Sext. alt.	Sextant altitude.
I.E.	Index Error (*Minus* if the ON reading is the greater).
Obs. alt.	Observed altitude.
Corrn.	Nautical Tables. (Sun's total corrn.) Plus.
True alt.	True altitude.
T.Z.D.	90° minus true altitude.
C.Z.D.	angle from natural haversine (xi).

Intercept *AWAY* if T.Z.D. is greater than C.Z.D. and vice versa.

Mnemonic:—
T A G

If T.Z.D. is the Greater intercept is Away.
(Otherwise, it is *TOWARDS*)

S.T.B. Sun's True Bearing from Weir's Diagram or Azimuth Tables, using (i), (ii) and (iii).

6: CORRESPONDENCE

It is essential that the style of a letter must be correct according to the type of letter it is desired to write.

There are three types of letters used in the Service:—
  (1) The Formal Service Letter.
  (2) The Communication or Headed Sheet.
  (3) A Private letter to a Senior Officer.

(1) The Formal Service Letter.
This is written on the following occasions:—
  (a) Acknowledgements of Appointments.
  (b) Reports of H.M. Ships' Proceedings.
  (c) Personal applications and requests.
  (d) Notifications (i.e., change of address or falling sick whilst on shore).
  (e) Suggestions and submissions on matters affecting the Welfare of the Service.
  (f) Letters to British Ministers, Consuls, etc.
  (g) Applications for Courts Martial, or Disciplinary Courts.

Example 1.   16, Elgin Gardens,
                                             Woking, Surrey.
Sir,   20th July, 1943.

   I have the honour to submit that I am sick on shore at the above address.

(2) Whilst leaving my home at 1730 to take up my appointment to H.M. Ship under your command, I slipped on the stairs causing injury to my right ankle.

(3) A telegram was sent immediately to you regarding this matter. In the temporary absence of the Naval Surgeon and Agent, my doctor was called in to attend to me.

(4) The Doctor pronounced that I am unfit to travel. He gave me a Medical Certificate, which I am enclosing herewith.

(5) I will take up my appointment as soon as the Doctor says that I am fit to travel, and until then, I will despatch a Certificate to you each week.

                I have the honour to be,
                   Sir,
                      Your obedient Servant,

                         . . . .
The Commanding Officer,   Sub. Lieut. R.N.V.R.
H.M.M.T.B. 66,
c/o G.P.O., London.

Example 2.   *Address.*
                                          Date.

Sir,

I have the honour to acknowledge receipt of my appointment to
H.M. Ship under your command to date . . . . (here insert the date of
taking up the appointment).

My address will be as above (*or as detailed*).

I have the honour to be

Sir,

Your obedient Servant,

. . . .

Sub. Lieut. R.N.V.R.

The Commanding Officer,
H.M.M.L. 89,
c/o G.P.O., London.

────────────

Notes:—

1. All paragraphs are numbered after the first.
2. The addressee is written at the foot of the first page, on the left.
3. When typing a letter, use double spaces.
4. In an acknowledgement of appointment, it is not necessary to
put the time and date of arrival—these are understood.
5. The letter is always to be addressed to the Commanding Officer,
never to a 'name' or individual.

────────────

(2) The Communication or Headed Sheet.

All Service matters except those covered by the Formal Service
letter are dealt with by this method.

Example 1.

From: The Commanding Officer, H.M.M.T.B. 66.
Date: 20th July, 1943.   No. 56/A/43.
To: The Commanding Officer, H.M.S. Bulldog.
Subject: John Smith, A.B., O. No. P/JX14897.
Recommendation for re-engagement.

It is requested that it may be confirmed that whilst in H.M.S.
Bulldog, the above-named rating was recommended for re-
engagement, as no such notation is shown on his Service Certificate
or Conduct Sheet.

(2) Documents are enclosed.

. . . .

Sub-Lieut. in Command.

MINUTE II.

No. 46/18/43.
H.M.M.T.B. 66.

This is confirmed and the necessary additions have been made on the Service Certificate and Conduct Sheet.
. . . .

H.M.S. Bulldog.   Lieutenant in Command.
22nd July, 1943.

Example 2.

From: The Commanding Officer, H.M.M.G.B. 76
Date: 22nd July, 1943.   *No.* 89/d/43.
To: Senior Officer, H.M.S. 'St. Christopher.'
  Subject: Issue of Inflatable life-belts.

Submitted,

On both occasions of the last two drafts joining H.M. Ship under my command, it was ascertained that the ratings were not in possession of inflatable life-belts.

(2) It is suggested, therefore, that in future, drafts for H.M. Ships may be issued with their life-belts before leaving their Bases or Depots, thus eliminating the delay and inconvenience caused both to the ship and to the Base from which the ship is operating.
. . . .

                                          Lieutenant in Command.

MINUTE II.

No. 96/6.
H.M.M.G.B. 78

This has been approved and passed to the appropriate authority for promulgation to all Establishments for necessary action in future.
. . . .

                        Commander (For Captain on leave).

H.M.S. 'St. Christopher.'
24th July, 1943.

Notes:—

1. Show the subject matter in the heading.
2. Separate letters are to be written on separate subjects.
3. Reply to a communication sheet either by a separate sheet or by minutes, as above.
4. When signing a letter for a Senior Officer on leave, the fact is to be stated as per second example.
5. Consult K.R. and A.I. Art. 879 (Returns and Correspondence).

(3) **A Private Letter to a Senior Officer.**

This is written in the same manner as to any other person whom you know.

Example 1.

> *Address.*
> *Date.*

Dear Commander Jones,

I should be grateful if you could arrange for my sextant which I left onboard to be forwarded to the above address.

I hope you will forgive me bothering you, but you told me to write to you in any case of difficulty.

I have been appointed to a command at last, an M.T.B., and I am enjoying it greatly. I should like to take the opportunity of thanking you for all that you did for me, and all that you taught me while I was in your ship. With the experience I have gained, I feel quite confident of making a success of this job.

> Yours sincerely,
> . . . .
> Lieut. R.N.V.R.

Note:—The same type of letter would be written in the case of a First Lieut. (a Sub Lieut.) writing to his Captain (a Lieutenant) who is on leave while his ship is undergoing a refit.

Example 2.

> H.M.M.L. 64,
> C/o G.P.O.,
> London
> 22nd July, 1943.

Dear Lieutenant Smith,

I tried to 'phone you yesterday evening, but you were out, and as it wasn't very important I didn't try again—a letter will do just as well.

The refit is going along quite well, and they are up to schedule, in fact I rather think they will finish a day or so ahead. However, I will let you know in due course about that.

I managed to get them to shift the compass two feet over to the port side as you wished; but I had quite a job to stop them from moving your bunk over to the other side of the cabin. You mentioned that there was a possibility of them wanting to do that, anyway, I don't think that they will try it again!

There is nothing of any further interest. The conduct of the Ship's Company is well up to standard, except that Fullglass came onboard drunk yesterday night. The Senior Officer of the Base gave him one day's pay stopped. As you know, it was his first offence, so I think that the punishment fitted the bill alright.

I hope you are enjoying your well earned leave, and that the weather is serving you better than it did me. Have a good time, and I hope to see you on Friday.

Yours sincerely,

. . . .

S/Lt. R.N.V.R.

Notes:—

1. Always start the letter with Dear, then the rank of the Officer, and his surname—nothing else.

2. Always end with, 'Yours sincerely,' never 'Yours faithfully,' 'truly,' etc.

3. Never splash the letter with 'Sir,' the word is not necessary.

Finally, and above all, keep your correspondence up-to-date. When you are going to write a letter, think what type is required, and adhere strictly to it as shown in the above example.

CHAPTER II
NOTES FOR MEDICAL OFFICERS
ON ENTRY INTO THE ROYAL NAVY

These notes are designed to give you an idea of what to expect and what is expected of you when you are appointed to a ship.

UNIFORM

You will need two suits of 'blues,' i.e. monkey jacket and trousers, and it is wise to choose a tailor who is familiar with the details of naval dress. Black shoes without toe caps, uniform cap, uniform raincoat without belt, white shirts, white collars, black tie and black socks complete the 'rig' (No.5). It is necessary to buy only a minimum of these accessories, for you can get more, and at much less cost, together with underclothing, pyjamas and so on, from naval stores after you have joined. As you may at any moment be sent to the tropic, you will need 'tropical rig' (A.F.O.1372/41), and your tailor will know all the details of this; but again do not buy more than is absolutely necessary, for you will be able to supplement your wardrobe either from naval stores, or from native tailors who make cheaply, quickly and well. There is no need to buy sea-boots or thick overcoats, as such gear can usually be supplied 'on loan' from naval stores. You may take your golf clubs, tennis racket and your favourite books, etc., but you must understand that in the event of loss compensation cannot be awarded from Naval funds in respect of the loss of any articles which are not essential to enable you to perform your Naval duties. You are advised that the question of insurance against such loss is one which you should consider in your own interests.

TRAVEL

You will receive a railway warrant, to enable you to take up your appointment, but you should keep account of incidental expenses, as a reasonable amount will be refunded, if you apply to the Pay Office after you have arrived. Every big station has a Railway Transport Officer, who will advise you if you are in difficulties, and if on arrival at your destination you are in doubt what to do next, go to the C. in C.'s or Senior Naval Officer's office and enquire where your ship is and how to get there. Your journey will be a good deal easier if your luggage is of such a size that you can carry it yourself if necessary.

THE SHIP

For practical purposes ships are of two sizes—small ships, such as a destroyer or a minesweeper in which you will be the only Medical Officer, or big ships, such as battleships, aircraft carriers, cruisers or armed merchant cruisers in which you will be one of two, three or possibly four Medical Officers. Your duties will vary accordingly, but one of the most important is to learn your way about your ship unerringly no matter what the difficulties or conditions. You cannot consider yourself efficient until you know what each compartment is, what goes on and who lives, works or sleeps in it. Make a point of seeing these places both by day and by night. It is natural to be a little shy of walking into what are, after all, men's homes, but there is a convention that 'If an Officer passing through a mess during stand-easy, meal hours, etc., carries his cap under his arm, it will indicate that no attention, other than clearing a gangway, is required' ('Running a Big Ship on Ten Commandments.' Rory O'Conor). If men rise at your entry, the order 'Carry on, please' will put them at ease, and it is then simple enough to ask any one, but preferably the Senior Petty Officer or Leading Hand present, any question you wish.

PERSONAL RELATIONSHIPS

Naval Officers are extraordinarily polite. Of whatever rank, they invariably address those senior to them as 'Sir,' and on formal occasions, as when the Admiral's 'Alert' is sounded, or a Captain is being piped over the side, all on deck come to attention. When boats are being used from ship to ship or ship to shore, the custom is that the senior Officers get down into the boat last and get out first. This will not come naturally to you at first, but if, for instance, you are going ashore for a round of golf with the Captain, and the Officer of the Watch reports 'Boat's alongside, Sir,' you should move off and get into the boat *before* the Captain, who will come last of all. On arrival, the Captain will get out first, and the other officers will follow in order of seniority.

The Navy's replies to invitations are delightfully simple—W.M.P. (with much pleasure), or M.R.U. (much regret unable), to R.P.C. (request the pleasure of your company).

CAPTAIN

Very shortly after your arrival on board, you will be presented to the Commanding Officer, who, whatever his rank, is always referred to as the Captain. Each day, on first sighting him, your 'Good morning, Sir,' if in the open air, should be accompanied by a formal salute; thereafter you may pass him without saluting, though naturally you will salute on joining or leaving him on occasions of duty. You rise when he enters the Ward Room, and you remove your cap when you enter his cabin. In your Service contact with him, you should understand that he alone is responsible for the health of the Ship's company, and that you are appointed to be his adviser in that department. You should therefore consult him upon any change of policy, which you think desirable, and obtain his approval before putting it into effect. In putting forward your ideas, try to foresee all the consequences, and have your answers ready to any objections which may be raised; and remember that a complaint against some present arrangement is of very little use unless it be accompanied by a practical suggestion for a remedy. You should report the state of health of the Ship's Company to the Captain daily (K.R. & A.I. 1407), and in your diagnosis and prognosis of particular cases endeavour to be as definite as possible: 'I've no idea, Sir,' is a most unsatisfactory answer to an enquiry of the probable length of an officer's illness or absence. If you receive a message 'The Captain would like to see you, Sir,' you must go at once; but if the message adds 'at your convenience,' the meaning is 'Finish what you are doing now, and then come and see me.' Remember that in war time, the Captain of a ship bears immense responsibilities; a discerning, and tactful Medical Officer can often do a good deal in small ways to help such a man.

SENIOR MEDICAL OFFICER

This Officer's courtesy title in a big ship is 'P.M.O.,' and your professional relationship to him is exactly that of a houseman to his honorary. He may, if he thinks you fit for it, leave you a good deal of initiative in the treatment of patients, but you must realise that he takes full responsibility for everything that happens in his department, and it is therefore up to you never to let him down. If you are in any doubt about a case, you should ask his advice. It may easily happen that you will disagree with him on some point or other, but once he has made his decision, you must accept it and implement it as loyally as though it were your own. Lose no opportunity of calling on the Medical Officers-in-Charge of hospitals, or on the Medical Officer of another ship; such preliminary contacts will prove of great value if you find yourself suddenly sent over to lend a hand in some emergency. Do not hesitate to ask them for technical information. If you learn that he has recently dealt with a number of casualties, get the story or ask for the loan of his Journal or special report. He will be glad to let you have it if you guarantee to return it.

OTHER OFFICERS

Take an interest in them; get to know them, where they are and what they do at Action Stations. Sooner or later, in a small ship, you will be consulted, not necessarily about their health but often about their family affairs, by nearly all of them; and remember that they are observing you closely, well knowing that at any moment their lives may be in your hands. A higher standard of personal conduct is expected of a Medical Officer than of any other. Read if you can a last-war book, 'Years of Endurance'—J. R. Muir.

RATINGS

Note that Chief and Petty Officers are always to be addressed with their titles (K.R. & A.I. 514.2), thus, not 'Brown, I want so and so,' but 'Petty Officer Brown, I want so and so.' Learn the significance of the badges on the sleeve and the ribbons on the coat. The great secret of control is to know the men, and this is made enormously easier if you can at the critical moment *name* the man, to whom you speak. You can produce order out of chaos almost in a moment by direct instructions to particular individuals by name. 'Er' and 'Hi' and 'You' are *not* effective.

SICK BERTH STAFF

The relationship between you and your Sick Berth staff is of course primarily that between any Officer and any rating, but there is also the normal relationship between a doctor and a nurse. In addition your Sick Berth rating is, in a sense, your confidential clerk or secretary and, if he is experienced, he will be able to give you considerable assistance in such things as forms and regulations. The principle that the best use must be made of the available men and material is particularly applicable to your own Sick Berth staff. If a man is inefficient, you must do your utmost to train him, and you should on no account attempt to get him relieved, until it is certain that all your efforts are in vain. Do not 'run him in' to Executive authority except as a last resort, for he is bound to lose face, and the Ship's Company's confidence in the man on whom, next to yourself, their medical care devolves.

PROFESSIONAL ABILITY

The greater your skill and the wider your interests the better. Can you put a temporary stopping in a tooth? Can you give a decent anæsthetic in the tropics with the minimum of apparatus? Can you be sure of spotting malarial parasites in a blood film you have stained yourself? How would you set about disinfecting the water in a large canvas bath? What do you know about the effects of blast, of the treatment of phosphorus burns, or of immersion foot? An endless list.

PROFESSIONAL RETICENCE

You should regard any information which may come into your possession in the course of your professional duties as strictly confidential. This attitude, which is based on ordinary professional etiquette, is of even more importance in the Service.

ORDERS

You must acquire a good working knowledge of K.R. & A.I. You should ask for Captain's Standing Orders, the Ship's War Orders, and the appropriate Station Orders, if no one happens to think of handing them to you. There are two series of weekly orders which you must scan carefully, A.F.O.'s and C.A.F.O.'s, for most important recommendations are published in them. It is also interesting and valuable to consult the A.F.O. Index and to look up previous orders on medical subjects. On arrival in a new port, you must run through the local 'General Orders' and 'Temporary Memoranda' as soon as possible, for they will contain up-to-date instructions on what precautions are to be taken to prevent diseases locally prevalent, and on the disposal of cases you wish to send to hospital. Get a copy of the 'Self-evident Code for use with Hospital Ships.' You should read the Manual of Instructions for the R.N. Sick Berth Staff and First Aid in the Royal Navy (B.R.25/43). There are many other publications of great value and interest. Those issued by the Admiralty include a Confidential Book on certain drugs, (C.B.3062); 'Advice to Medical Officers in Ships on Psychiatric Cases and Casualties,' (B.R.898/42); 'The Treatment of Battle Casualties Afloat,' (B.R.143/42); C.B.04211; two little pamphlets on the treatment of Head Injuries, (B.R.148/40 and 114/41); and 'The Use of the Eyes at Night,' a reprint of an American publication. The journal of the Royal Naval Medical Service appears once a quarter. The War Office has issued 'Resuscitation,' and a note 'Concerning the Use of Sulphonamide Derivatives.' You should read also 'Medical Care of Flying Personnel in War,' (A.167116/41

D.G.M.S.); 'Neuroses in War Time,' sponsored by the Ministry of Pensions, and the series of War Memoranda issued by the Medical Research Council. If a C.B. is drawn a signature must be given for it and when it is returned you must get a signature for it yourself or see that your signature is cancelled. The loss of a C.B. is a serious matter—full regulations for handling them are in C.B. Form U.2.D.

WHERE TO APPLY FOR BOOKS OF REFERENCE

C.Bs.	Ship's C.B. Officer.
C.A.F.Os., A.F.Os., Captain's orders, Ship's War Orders and K.R & A.I.	Captain's Secretary.
Station Orders, Local Orders and Temporary Memoranda ...	Captain's Secretary.
B.Rs. and O.Us.	Captain's Secretary.

CORRESPONDENCE

The simplest method of writing to Senior Officers is to use a Communication Sheet, the headings on which state clearly who is writing, on what date, to whom. Letters should always be written to the head of the establishment and sub-headed to the departmental officer concerned; next indicate the subject, followed by the single word 'Submitted,' which means 'Please give this your attention.' So you begin like this:—

> From:—Medical Officer, H.M.S. 'Nonesuch.'
> Date:—1st January, 1950.
> To:—M.O. i/c R.N.H., Port Blank,
>   for Senior Pharmacist.
>   Subject:—Additional stores for H.M.S. 'Nonesuch.'
> Submitted:—

Now comes the text of your letter, ending with your signature and rank. This gets rid of inappropriate terms, such as 'Dear Sir' and 'Your sincerely.' The only exception is in writing direct to M.D.G., through your Captain, to whom you begin 'Sir, I have the honour to report, etc.,' and end 'I have the honour to be,

>   Sir,
>   Your obedient Servant,
>   *A. N. Other.*
>   Surgeon Lieutenant, R.N.V.R.'

Any Service letter that you write, except the purely departmental *must* be shown to the Captain (K.R. & A.I.875 & 1363). It is often convenient to continue a correspondence on the same sheet, thus if you receive a note saying in effect 'What's become of the M.H.S.?', you reply 'II. I sent it to hospital with him.' Then if they say, 'III. It isn't there,' you say 'IV. It should be—see my II above.' Write clearly and briefly, not 'In the event of an accident of a serious nature occurring,' but 'If there is a serious accident.' If you wish to write for the Press, you must be very careful to obey the orders on that subject (vide Art. 17 K.R. & A.I.).

FORMS

The best way of dealing with these (see the list on page 19 of 'Scale of Medicines, Instruments, etc., for Service Afloat') is to construct a diagram showing the patient's progress through the Sick Bay and indicating the necessary forms at each stage. On being put 'Sick' he must be noted in the Daily Sick List, M.195, and later in M.179g, part of the Journal; the Captain, the Divisional Officer and the Coxswain should be informed. If the illness is infectious, S.576 is appropriate for venereal disease, S.220 for tubercle, higher authorities being informed on M.75 (S.1123). If his sickness is caused by an injury, M.183 may be necessary, and in either case a note must be made on S.446, the Medical History Sheet. If he has to be sent to hospital, his M.H.S., a Sick Voucher S.47, and an M.188, Case of a Patient Invalided, Dead, or sent to Hospital, must accompany him. A note must be made on M.184 if you supply a truss, on M.177a if you prescribe a dangerous drug, and on M.201 for a dental appointment. If your diagram is displayed in a conspicuous position in the Sick Bay, it will prevent you or your staff overlooking these details.

JOURNALS

Your Journal (K.R. & A.I. 1410) should be meticulously accurate; careful study of the 'Instructions' will make it so, and will prevent mistakes, whose correction gives much unnecessary trouble. The classification of injuries is not, at first glance, very clear. A wound or injury in action is in a class by itself and may require a special report (A.F.Os. 2698/42 and 3627/42). Other injuries necessitating treatment on the Sick List are to be put either under General Injuries or under Local Injuries, in the appropriate subdivision. A minor injury, therefore, is by definition (K.R. & A.I. 1386.3) one that does not require treatment on the Sick List, and need only be noted on M. 187h. Thus, from the point of view of the Nosological return, M. 179d. of your Journal, when a man breaks his wrist by a fall outside the precincts of dockyard, docks, jetty or liberty boat, the injury is then a local injury 'not on duty other causes,' but if he is within the precincts of the dockyard, docks, jetty or liberty boat and is sober, the injury is regarded as a 'local injury on duty.' Again, a man who barks his shin on a hatch combing on his way to 'Payment,' and later, developing an ulcer, has to be treated for a few days on the Sick List, must come out of the Minor Injury List, in which probably you originally put him, and be shown as 'Local Injury, on duty, Employment.'

MEDICAL STORES

In a ship you will receive primarily an issue of medical stores on the 'Service Afloat' scale. Should you feel that you require some additional instrument, drug etc., do not hesitate to apply to the most convenient medical store depot giving your reasons for the demand, which, if reasonable, will be given sympathetic consideration. In this connection you must remember that there is not a super-abundance of instruments, and you cannot expect to find your ship equipped like the hospital which you have left.

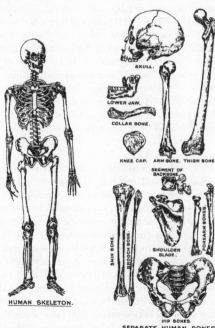

HUMAN SKELETON.

SKULL.
LOWER JAW.
COLLAR BONE.
KNEE CAP. ARM BONE. THIGH BONE.
SEGMENT OF BACKBONE.
SHIN BONE.
BROOCH BONE.
FOREARM BONES.
SHOULDER BLADE.
HIP BONES.
SEPARATE HUMAN BONES.

Do not let yourself be carried away by manufacturers' advertisements and articles in the lay, or even medical, press about such therapeutic measures as ultra-violet light, vitamins, proprietary drugs, etc., which may have a known value but should not be demanded until you have satisfied yourself critically that they are essential for the good of your patients. Remember that it is not possible to provide X-ray units and microscopes to every ship and you must learn to come to decisions on occasions by clinical acumen without reference to a laboratory, X-ray department, etc., which perhaps in your previous experience were readily available.

You should not take expensive privately owned instruments with you to a ship. Should they be lost you cannot expect to receive compensation except for such essential personal items as a stethoscope, or perhaps a diagnostic set. The same applies to books. Ideally every ship carrying a medical officer should have a small library, but this is not practicable. You are likely to be compensated only for the loss of such books as are comparable with those which would be included in the 'Service Afloat' medical library, and if such a library is in the ship compensation for loss cannot be expected.

Should you not have an electric steriliser, or the one which you have breaks down, do not forget that there are homelier methods of sterilisation available. Do all in your power to render your store accounts accurately. This may seem a tedious task in time of war, but some check must be kept. In particular make certain that your expenditure of dangerous drugs is most accurately recorded. Your difficulties are well realised, but the effort can be made.

If you are short of any stores on your specified scale, or feel that you do need additional items, do not sit feeling aggrieved and do nothing, like a good many do, but, when the opportunity arises, ask.

MEDICAL ORGANISATION

Perhaps, when you join your small ship, you will take over from another Medical Officer, who will show you round and explain his routine arrangements. There will be forms to sign for stores transferred, and not enough time to go into every detail. As soon as possible, however, you will make yourself familiar with everything committed to your charge. You ought to read also that part of the Geneva Convention, which defines the position of Medical Officers. It is a constant source of regret to Junior Medical Officers that their clinical work is so much restricted, but there is a good deal of preventive medicine (see C.A.F.O.882/41), and it is most important to keep up to date with inoculations, (A.F.O. 1003/42), and vaccinations. You will find, too, that serious cases come to you at a very early stage, so much so that may you occasionally be tempted, when abnormal physical signs cannot be detected, to fancy that the patient is malingering. This is liable to lead to mortifying errors in diagnosis. It is very much better that a malingerer should get away with it for a day or two than that a serious illness should be missed, and you must take good care that your judgment is not biased by those who have no qualification to give an opinion.

ALCOHOLISM

When you are requested to examine a man thought to be drunk (K.R. & A.I.462a and 1135.9), bear in mind that it is not your business to decide whether he is drunk or not, but you must be prepared, as a result of your examination, to say whether he is suffering from alcoholism, or from some other disease or injury, or from a combination of both; and if you are asked, you may give your opinion on whether he is fit for duty. The Executive Officer having received your report, will decide the question of drunkenness. Nevertheless, it is a mistake to be lenient simply from compassion, for if a semi-intoxicated man, instead of being safely stowed down below until he has recovered, is allowed freedom, he may easily commit another offence, such as 'striking,' and will then be in very serious trouble. For a lucid summary of what is required in medical evidence, see Notes on pp. 60-61, 'Admiralty Memorandum on Court-Martial Procedure.'

ACTION STATIONS

What is expected of you is clearly stated in B.R.143/42, and the Admiralty policy of dispersal, both of medical men and of medical stores, is fully discussed in A.F.O. 1489/42. It is easy to get extra wooden boxes made on board, and painted black with a conspicuous Red Cross, for distribution throughout the ship; every large compartment should have some such provision. Before you begin to lecture on First Aid, (A.F.O.3110/42), and give your remarkable demonstration of the difference between arterial and venous bleeding with the aid of an ear syringe and a piece of rubber tubing, you should consider not so much what would be ideal as what is going to be possible under 'Action' conditions. You must convince officers and men alike that this is a most important matter and that their personal responsibility for First Aid treatment is paramount. It is a good idea to put down in black and white exactly what you expect of them in an emergency. These notes of yours should stress the necessity of wearing identity discs and anti-flash gear, of knowing where First Aid containers and Neil Robertson stretchers are, and of providing in suitable places ample supplies of drinking water and sweet tea, to which half a teaspoonful of common salt to the pint has been added. Indicate where you and your skilled assistants will be stationed, stress the danger of an unnecessary or improperly applied tourniquet, and explain the harm likely to be done by unwise movement of badly wounded men. The principle that First Aid must be given on the spot must be explicitly stated, and the following headings may be useful:—

1. Stop the bleeding—a tourniquet is only to be used for spurting arteries. All other bleeding will be sufficiently arrested if you apply a first field or other dressing, with extra cotton wool if necessary, and bandage widely and firmly.
2. Look for other injuries.
3. Protect from cold.
4. Give drinks if possible, but *not* to a man wounded in the belly or unconscious.

When these notes are complete, submit them to the Captain, and if he approves, have a number of copies made and distribute them freely. You must plan in your own mind exactly how you are going to deal with a large number of burns, and you must have a ready-made, but sufficiently elastic, scheme for handling numbers of casualties transferred to you from other ships, or picked up from the water. One such scheme would be to take over a large mess-deck as a temporary ward, and to allot to each casualty one of your own Ship's Company as 'nurse,' saying to him, 'Smith, here's your patient, lay him down there, get some blankets for him, undress him as gently as possible and clean him up; give him something to drink (bearing in mind No. 4 above), and make him as comfortable as you can. I'll be along to look at his injuries as soon as you are ready.'

OTHER DUTIES AND INTERESTS

Every Ward Room Officer does something for the general welfare in addition to his special job. You will probably be 'lurked' for censoring or catering. You may, if you show any aptitude, be asked to be Sports Officer or Broadcast Commentator. Any recreation or entertainment, which you can devise to relieve monotony and tedium, will be of great value to and much appreciated by the Ship's Company. As time goes on, you will find that in their eyes you, as a Medical Officer, stand a little apart from other Officers. Where all are concerned for their welfare, it is one of your special interests, and your personal contacts in the Sick Bay, and perhaps your censoring duties also, will give you a very good idea of what the men are thinking and how they are 'taking it.'

You are at the beginning of a fine adventure and of new experiences. No one is 'behind the lines' in a ship nowadays, and you will share all risks and dangers equally with your brother officers and men. This is a great privilege. Strive ever to be worthy of it.

CHAPTER III

THE TREATMENT OF BATTLE CASUALTIES AFLOAT

1: INTRODUCTION AND MEDICAL ORGANISATION

During the past twenty years surgery has so rapidly advanced that no single individual can be a master of all its branches. When the duties of a naval surgeon after an action at sea are considered, the additional limitations enforced by surrounding conditions can be easily understood. Under the most favourable circumstances emergency surgery alone may be attempted; yet it is remarkable what successful results may accrue if the right procedure is carried out at the right time on the healthy bluejacket who is in the prime of life.

Two incidents which occurred in H.M.S. *Victory* at the Battle of Trafalgar provide us at once with a contrast and a resemblance to our practice of to-day. After Lord Nelson had been wounded on the quarter-deck, he was carried to the cockpit four decks below—the man-handling entailed must have grievously exaggerated the shock from his injuries! Sir William Beatty describes the musket ball which killed Lord Nelson thus: 'On removing the ball a portion of the gold lace and pad of the epaulette together with a small piece of his lordship's coat, was found firmly attached to it.' From the surgical aspect precisely the same event is repeated when the blue serge or flannel of the sailor is dragged through the wound by a shell splinter.

The scope of the surgeon's activities will be measured to some extent by the type of ship in which he is serving. For example, a Medical Officer in a small ship can perform relatively little surgery compared with that possible in a battleship or battle-cruiser carrying three or more Medical Officers and half a dozen sick-berth staff. On the other hand the heavy type of ship can bear punishment better, and her large complement may suffer more casualties. In any case a sound Medical Officer will study in detail the construction of the ship to which he is appointed. He should be well acquainted with the numbers and position of the main bulkheads, the hatches and the water-tight doors which are open or closed during action, the precise situation of the fresh-water tanks and main ventilating trunks. Such advice may appear redundant in times of peace; on the other hand, the havoc wrought by an explosive shell between decks will often render the task of reaching the wounded in the darkness extremely difficult.

The layout and organisation of the medical department in ships must be adaptable to both peace-time and war-time conditions and include:—

(1) Skilled treatment for the wounded and sick.
(2) Provision of accommodation, food, clothing, warmth, nursing and medical comforts.
(3) The training of personnel in First Aid and the provision of stretcher parties.
(4) Arrangements for the transport of casualties.
(5) Organisation for action—quick changes from normal peace-time arrangements centralised in the Sick Bay, to a widely dispersed system of medical posts.

To appreciate this policy every Medical Officer must be conversant with KR. and A.I. Article 1395; C.B. 4198/R. (Handbook of Damage Control); and A.F.O. 1489/42.

PEACE—A CENTRALISED SYSTEM

Normally the greater part of a ship's 15-20 years' service may be spent at peace; even during periods of hostilities much of the time may be occupied far away from scenes of enemy activity.

The Admiralty adheres to the long declared policy of a Sick Bay in the upper part of the ship, convenient to main living and working spaces and sited where the amenities of natural light and ventilation are available. Thus it can fit into the ship's routine and carry out the function of a small modern hospital to the best advantage.

In war this exposed position is extremely vulnerable, and it becomes necessary to provide a more protected place to which existing sick can be quickly transferred and where casualties can be received.

WAR—PROVISION FOR ACTION
Decentralisation. Development of Distributing Stations (D/S); Introduction of the First Aid Post (F.A.P.).

Up to the present war, organisation for action had been governed by a rigid interpretation of K.R. and A.I. Article 1395. In larger ships this consisted in evacuating the Sick Bay to Distributing Stations situated in protected positions, which merely acted as places of refuge for medical stores and personnel. Pending a lull in the action casualties could receive only minimal first aid locally, use being made of first field dressings, etc., from haversacks previously distributed round the ship, e.g., at gun stations, in the engine room, etc. When the action was over, the Sick Bay, if still serviceable, reverted to its ordinary function; otherwise some upper deck space had to be chosen where the casualties could be given more methodical treatment.

Gradually the Distributing Stations (D/S) came to be looked upon as the places where the wounded should be mustered; but to satisfy the requirements for 'best possible protection,' they were often deep down in the ship and could only be reached with consid-erable difficulty. The compartments were inadequately fitted and no special provision was made for retaining cot cases.

Experience during the first year of hostilities showed that to meet new forms of warfare there was great need for improvement upon the above traditional arrangements. A more flexible organisation was required for wider dispersal of medical personnel and equipment to ensure better facilities for the reception and treatment of casualties.

Enemy attacks, e.g., from the air, may persist over many hours, and places must be

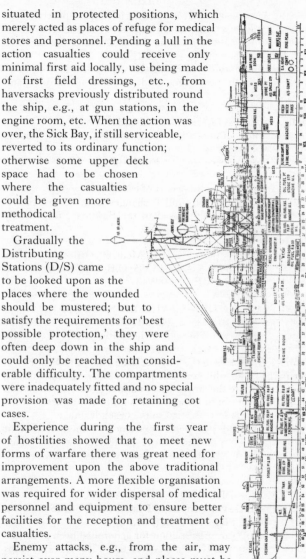

available during this time where wounded can be accommodated and given urgent surgical treatment. The efficiency of the previous scheme also suffered from the wide hiatus between the first aid haversacks and the D/S. There arose a demand for subsidiary medical posts in convenient positions throughout the ship, which would bring skilled assistance nearer scenes of casualty and obviate the difficulties and dangers of excessive stretcher work.

To meet these requirements it became necessary to alter and extend the existing organisation in the following ways:—each Distributing Station was given a wider role, and the system of First Aid Posts was introduced; in addition to being a place of refuge and a safe deposit for medical stores the D/S becomes a satellite Sick Bay in case the Sick Bay proper is rendered untenable. The compartment is fitted to allow for emergency operations, and to accommodate wounded for considerable periods during prolonged intermittent attack.

(399/2839)   A#3

Requirements of D/Ss. The D/S should be of adequate size, under protection and so situated that there is easy access for stretchers and sufficient room for treatment. It must be possible to bring cases there with a minimum of movement and discomfort. An approach through a series of angled passages, manholes and narrow tunnels is dangerous to the patient and renders the compartment entirely useless.

In many older vessels the place allocated is unsatisfactory or inadequate, and in certain types of new construction it may not have been found feasible to allocate a permanent D/S at all. Dependence must then be placed on earmarking some working or living space that can be adapted to the purpose in an emergency. A survey of the upper decks will reveal certain places which could be used by the surgeons after action (K.R. and A.I. 1395, 2 (*f*)). The choice of such sites is affected by the considerations described above.

A list, preferably typewritten or printed, is made of such sites and their contents, and a reserve of medical supplies set aside and labelled for use in them. This theoretical ideal may not be realisable owing to limitation of supplies; the valise is available in Flagships, and the khaki roll is being issued as widely as possible.

First Aid Posts. A study of the reports from ships confirms the soundness of the policy for this first-line system of casualty posts well scattered up and down the ship. This applies the 'dispersal' theory, and will ensure the most efficient medical service for battle.

The advantages of this distribution are as follows:—

(*a*) Reduction in loss of medical personnel and equipment.

(*b*) First Aid and temporary shelter for the wounded can be quickly obtained and rapid turnover of cases facilitated.

(*c*) Transport of untreated cases to distant parts of the ship is avoided.

(*d*) Lines of communication will not become obstructed by Stretcher Parties during action.

(*e*) Risk of added injury and shock to untreated cases is avoided by postponing removal to an operating station.

It is now agreed that the most imperative necessity in the immediate care of wounded is treatment of surgical shock. Shock is invariably present in severe injuries, but its presence must also be expected in cases of burns. Moving a badly shocked man, even by stretcher, is bound to have a deleterious effect on his condition, and if the movement is prolonged or effected without the greatest care and deliberation it is extremely likely to precipitate death. Therefore serious casualties should only be moved the shortest possible distance, pending recovery from shock. Hasty attempts to convey badly wounded men from exposed positions on the upper deck to D/Ss difficult of access below have resulted in many fatalities which might have been avoided. The jolting and twisting of wounded men through intricate passages and down vertical ladders can cause the greatest pain, complicate injuries, increase hæmorrhage and gravely jeopardise their chance of survival. First Aid, warmth and restoratives must be applied at the outset, and a period of rest must be allowed (usually about two hours is necessary) for the initial shock to pass off before the patient is carried to a main centre for completion of treatment.

Siting of First Aid Posts. The larger the ship the more numerous must be the places chosen as F.A.Ps. Four in number, port, starboard, fore and aft, will probably suffice in cruisers; but strict limitation to this number in a battleship will lead to congestion of traffic, delay in giving treatment and overcrowding of posts. The question is also affected by the number of medical staff and assistants available to man the posts: a party of two at least will be needed in each post, one being a Medical Officer, a Sick Berth rating or a specially qualified First Aid worker, the other a less skilled assistant.

It is important that the Senior Medical Officer should not be immobilised permanently at any one post. He should be able to move about as necessary, supervising and adjusting the organisation to meet changes in the situation as they arise.

The exact disposition of the F.A.Ps. is a matter of internal economy to be worked out as early as possible in the commission. To this end the ship could be divided into areas, each to have its own medical post as centre so that the whole vessel is adequately provided for. In choosing the exact sites special attention should be paid to:—

(1) Adequate working space.

(2) Blast and splinter-proof cover, and protection from weather.

(3) Ready access from action stations without obstructing other traffic and easy passage for stretchers.

(4) Good light and ventilation.

(5) Proximity to water supply and telephone.

(6) Presence of benches and tables adaptable to First Aid uses.

(7) Convenience for fitting bulkhead First Aid cupboard for dressings, splints, medical comforts, etc.

(8) Stowage for stretchers and reserve blankets.

Medical Officers of various ships have already selected the following sites as specially suitable for First Aid Posts in accordance with A.F.O. 1489/42, as conforming generally to the above requirements:—

Wardroom, Gunroom and Warrant Officers' mess, Captain's quarters, cabin flat, crew spaces, recreation room, reading room, schoolroom, chapel, dental surgery, canteen flat, laundry, torpedo parking space, upper deck bathrooms, the island and balloon space in Carriers, superstructure in Destroyers.

The approaches to these centres should be conspicuously marked in a uniform manner, e.g., with the words 'First Aid Posts' and a Red Cross, also with an arrow pointing the way. Everyone on board should know where these places are situated. Pending lulls in action to permit of their larger function, D/Ss. will act as F.A.Ps.

There should also be available in certain places First Aid haversacks, or preferably the metal containers now available in lieu (A.F.O. 3417/41) for use when it is not possible to make immediate use of the F.A.Ps.

Medical parties must take every opportunity (e.g., at practice action stations, etc.) to familiarise themselves with the exact location of, and quickest way of approach to, the different emergency posts, and with the routes for the transport of wounded. The possibility of many of these getting blocked in the course of the engagement must be remembered.

Instruction in First Aid. Every effort should be made to instruct the whole ship's company in Elementary First Aid. The essential

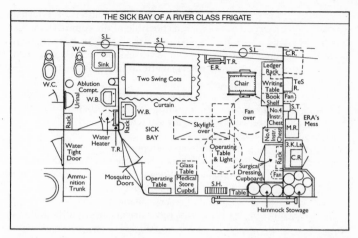

THE SICK BAY OF A RIVER CLASS FRIGATE

principles are few—arrest of severe hæmorrhage, clearing the respiratory airway, removing the casualty from the causative agent or vice versa, the provision of temporary cover and warmth and the immediate application of artificial respiration to the apparently drowned (there have been cases when this has been successful after 3 1/2 hours). The correct and expeditious application of these principles in the moment of crisis may be of at least as much value as skilful surgery after the event.

Personnel must also be impressed with the importance of wearing Anti-Flash Gear, and overalls if possible, and of lying flat on the deck when unoccupied.

PREPARATION FOR ACTION

(1) Evacuate the Sick Bay and its existing cot cases as necessary to D/Ss. or other pre-arranged places under the best protection available. The number of sick retained on board fighting ships in war time should be kept to a minimum, every opportunity being taken to transfer cases to hospital. Probably there will still be some Sick List to provide for, but it must be recognised that there is only limited accommodation in the emergency stations.

(2) Prepare and man D/Ss. and F.A.Ps. This is confined to the provision of as large a quantity of a few essential stores as the scale will admit, all preparations for major surgery or technique more elaborate than First Aid being confined to the provision of a chest or cupboard stocked with essentials for use after action.

The following stores are advised in large quantities:—

Triangular bandages. Elastoplast.

Lint and gauze, cotton wool (already available in the form of shell dressings).

Lengths of wood or malleable metal of varying sizes.

Pails or basins of disinfectant solution of a strength suitable for use on open wounds, e.g., acriflavine 1/1000.

Sulphanilamide powder. Sponges.

Lengths of rubber tubing for tourniquets.

Provision for suture of wounds and ligature to control hæmorrhage.

Tubes of anti-burn jelly or bottles of 10 per cent. tannic solution in 1/1000 acriflavine for the treatment of burns.

Blankets, hot bottles and hot drinks.

Morphia, which should usually be given in 1/2 grain doses; labelling is desirable but may be impracticable, in which case the appearance of the case must serve as a guide.

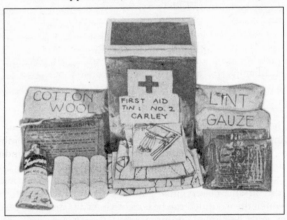

(3) Divide Medical Stores, apportioning the majority to the D/Ss. Allowance must be made for modern warfare and especially for underwater explosion, and consideration should be given in addition to the distribution of stores on the level of the upper deck both forward and aft. Emergency chest and First Aid requirements should be dispersed as widely as possible.

(4) Check First Aid bags (or metal containers) and make sure that they are in position and properly equipped.

(5) Distribute First Field and Shell Dressings to men in exposed and isolated positions.

(6) Distribute Neil Robertson and W.O. pattern stretchers in suitable places.

(7) Issue Tubunic Ampoules of Omnopon to Non-Medical Personnel (*see* A.F.O.994/42).

(8) Make arrangements for the supply of oatmeal water (*see* K.R. and A.I. 1825, para. 3 (*a*)) or sweet tea, hot or cold, to men at action stations, in an effort to minimise the shock consequent upon excessive sweating at their work.

(9) Prepare a supply of dry clothing for those who may be immersed in water or oil fuel.

Personal Equipment of the Surgeon. During action certain small essentials for treatment are easily lost in darkness and confusion. It is advisable to wear overalls with large pockets, to tie a pair of scissors and two artery forceps to the belt, pin a Wildeys Syringe to the chest, and carry a rubber-capped bottle of morphine sulphate, a length of rubber tubing (tourniquet), some First Field dressings and some labels in the pockets. A torch must be slung over the shoulder and a belt worn. Headlamps are also available and should be demanded in accordance with A.F.O. 2534/42.

DURING ACTION

Very little warning can be expected, and there is no certainty that the enemy will confine himself to any one form of attack. Combined methods are likely, and medical defence must be correspondingly well distributed. It is, for example, insufficient to 'Man D/Ss.' only, on the assumption that the attack will be limited to surface bombardment and heavy guns, and that frequent lulls will occur during which the wounded can be collected. All the dispersal medical positions must be named and prepared to receive casualties, render First Aid and retain cases until they can be safely moved by stretcher.

During action, conditions in the operating theatre are such that no serious surgical work can be attempted; the traditional silence is replaced by a confusing medley of sound—the roar of salvoes and shattering detonations as the ship gives and receives punishment, the din of Fire Parties clearing burning debris and of Repair Parties shoring up bulkheads and fixing temporary lighting between decks. There are the added discomforts of fumes, smoke and water, and the ship's evolutions will increase the extent and frequency of her roll and pitch.

While the ship is actually under fire it is probably only possible to shift wounded men to some cover out of the way of combatants and use First Aid haversacks. When opportunity offers Medical Parties from the F.A.Ps. may be able to render assistance and supervise moving of serious cases.

This is necessarily the occasion for Elementary First Aid to be given at once and on the spot by the men themselves. *The importance of giving thorough instruction in such methods beforehand cannot therefore be over-estimated.*

In modern warfare attack is likely to be continued for long periods, e.g.,, there may be incessant waves of aerial bombardment stretching over many hours, and the need for some places of temporary refuge is evident. During lulls in the fighting steps can be taken by the medical staff to sort cases, collect them to the nearest post by the use of stretchers over short distances, and proceed with urgent treatment. Walking cases can make their own way to a centre. It is not, however, until action is entirely over that Stretcher Parties can be employed to the full for removal of casualties along main passages, and to a place where operative measures will be undertaken.

AFTER ACTION

The situation should be reviewed and a decision made as to where the final casualty station and operating theatre are to be set up.

The Sick Bay or D/S may be available, but alternative positions will have already been considered (vide K.R. & A.I 1395, clauses 2 (e) and (f)), and a list of such positions should have appeared in Ships' Orders.

A suitable place, preferably aft on the upper deck, should have been earmarked for use as a mortuary.

Morphia must be given in full doses to all wounded before they are moved; all are labelled with the amount given at the time. When under the influence of this invaluable drug they are moved to the nearest place wherein they can be kept dry and warm. Those from the upper deck are taken below; those between decks may be placed on mess tables so as to be clear of the decks awash. The importance of diminishing initial wound shock by a minimum of manhandling cannot be over-estimated. Provision of hot drinks such as hot soup or cocoa is of great benefit.

When firing has ceased, decks and passages will be free from the traffic incidental to 'action stations.' Only then will it be possible to proceed with the clearing of casualties to the centres set aside for final treatment. At the same time it must be remembered that the enemy may renew his attack, and there may be a call for quick reversal to 'organisation during action.'

If the case can be transferred to hospital or hospital ship within a few hours of an action the need for active surgical intervention will be reduced to a minimum. The chief points to be borne in mind may be classified thus:—

(1) The treatment of shock.

(2) The careful treatment of burns of the exposed parts, such as face and hands.

(3) The accurate adjustment of splints and bandages for safe transit and prevention of secondary shock.

(4) The control of hæmorrhage, a sharp watch being kept for reactionary hæmorrhage.

(5) Repeated doses of morphia where necessary. To obtain the best results, morphia must be given till its effect is evident.

(6) The routine administration of anti-tetanic serum in all cases of wounding (*see* A.F.O. 3463/40).
Dosage:—
(*a*) If previously immunised one dose of 3,000 international units.
(*b*) If not immunised three doses of 3,000 international units at weekly intervals.
(*c*) In particularly dirty septic or extensive wounds the initial dose (or in the case of the immunised, the single dose) should be 6,000-9,000 international units.

(7) Anti-gas gangrene serum should be given when considered necessary (*see* A.F.O. 4672/41).

(8) The indications for the use of sulphonamide derivatives are shown in Part III and B.R. 109 (*see* A.F.O. 4672/41).

SCHAFER'S METHOD OF ARTIFICIAL RESPIRATION

2: TREATMENT WHERE FACILITIES ARE LIMITED

The Medical Officer in a small ship is expected to stay at his post unless summoned elsewhere in the ship for some special purposes; for example, to liberate a casualty who is pinned by a damaged portion of the ship, or to render First Aid to an Officer who cannot leave his post. A summons of doubtful authority should be answered by detailing a sick berth rating to investigate. The Medical Officer is required to do two things and two things only:—

(1) To administer skilled First Aid to the injured.
(2) By his manner of so doing, to reinforce the courage of the seriously wounded and re-establish the morale of those who may be more frightened than hurt.

This second most important duty he will best fulfil, not by thinking about it, but by proceeding methodically, quietly and without hurry about his first task, which will now be considered in more detail under the following heads:—

(1) Dressing of Wounds.
(2) Treatment of Burns.
(3) Arrest of Bleeding.
(4) Treatment of Shock.
(5) Delayed Treatment.

1. Dressing of Wounds. Casualties during and immediately after the action will reach the Medical Officer in two ways: (*a*) less severely wounded cases will find their own way, and may arrive with no dressings at all on wounds that are still bleeding; and (*b*) cases of graver injury will be assisted or carried to the dressing station; these cases are likely to have had some First Aid dressing already applied at the place in the ship where they were wounded.

To the first class of case he will apply the patient's own First Aid dressing, after ligaturing any spurting artery or twisting it with a pair of artery forceps, relying upon the pressure of the dressings to stop less severe bleeding. For these initial dressings gauze taken straight from the packet and moistened with flavine 1 in 1,000 can be used, or the wound may be lightly dusted with sulphanilamide powder (not more than a heaped teaspoonful being used *in toto*).

There is one type of wound which demands urgent attention—the open wound of the pleura or sucking wound of the chest. Such cases are of the gravest nature, and the life of the patient hangs upon their prompt and appropriate treatment. The wound should be at once closed by means of a rapidly performed suture of its edges, the stitches including in their grasp the skin and some of the underlying tissues, to ensure that they do not 'cut out.' An alternative method is to employ a vaseline or paraffin gauze pad, outside which is placed a piece of mackintosh or jaconet; the whole kept in position by means of several pieces of elastoplast. The wound is to be dusted with sulphanilamide powder before the insertion of the suture or the application of the emergency pack. No attempt should be made to irrigate wounds of the chest wall, or to apply lotions locally, owing to the danger of their entering the bronchial system through a fistula and acting as lung irritants.

Morphia should be administered at once by hypodermic injection; an initial dose of gr. 1/2 may be required to produce the effect desired, viz., abolition of pain for several hours. A label giving the time and dosage should be attached to every patient when morphia has been given.

2. First Aid Treatment of Burns. It is important to remember that no extensive local treatment of burns must be undertaken until the Medical Officer is satisfied that shock has been adequately treated; in the past valuable lives have been lost owing to extensive local treatment being undertaken before shock had been efficiently treated. As most war burns, especially if they involve the whole thickness of the skin, are very liable to become septic it is advisable to use a coagulant which has antiseptic properties. Anti-burn jelly, such as Gentian Violet jelly (1 per cent.) with merthiolate, should be applied liberally to the burnt surfaces. The gentian violet has a selective antiseptic action against gram-positive organisms, and an analgesic action which usually affords local relief of pain in a few minutes; a thin pliable tan is also produced.

Any attempt made to cleanse the burnt area by means of soap and water is unnecessary if the jelly is applied shortly after the receipt of the burn, since the heat which caused the burn must have rendered the area sterile for an hour or so. Blisters if present are snipped and dead skin is removed before the jelly is applied.

No dressings are applied whatever, thereby permitting delayed blisters to be opened and more jelly to be applied.

It may, however, be necessary to cover the burnt area with some gauze and a bandage if transport to hospital is undertaken.

Burns in the region of the eyes and lids are of special importance, and should be dressed with wet saline packs which are kept continually moist by the addition of fresh saline.

3. Arrest of Bleeding has already been considered under Section 1. Casualties brought with an improvised tourniquet in position should, if bleeding has been arrested, be noted of early attention; the tourniquet should not be interfered with until all the casualties have been seen once, or until there is a decided lull in their arrival. For the later treatment of such cases *see* Paragraph 5.

4. Treatment of Shock. This is fully described in B.R. 110, 'The Treatment of Wound Shock' (M.R.C. War Memorandum No. 1) and B.R. 22 War Office publication on 'Resuscitation.'

The first and most important step in the combating of shock will have been taken when every patient is under the influence of an adequate dose of *morphia*. The next step is to secure *dryness and warmth*. Water from firehoses, burst pipes or coming in-board may make the deck of the dressing station wet, and a dry berth for the casualties may be difficult or impossible to secure until alternative accommodation is put at the disposal of the Medical Officer, or until cots or stretchers can be slung in previously prepared rope slings. Temporary use may be made of settees, tables, etc. While casualties are left on the deck, the feet, not the head, should be placed towards the bulkhead to avoid any possible concussion.

5. Delayed Treatment. This comprises the second stage of the skilled first-aid. When all the casualties have been dressed, are under morphia,* are dry and in process of being warmed, it is the duty of the Medical Officer to go round the whole number methodically. His object will be to deal with any reactionary bleeding which may have started, to re-dress and thus learn more in detail about the wounds, to discover others overlooked in the first instance and to splint fractures. Whilst so engaged, he will see that hot drinks are prepared and given freely to all except those with an abdominal wound.

In the event of many casualties considerable judgment will be required in deciding the order in which they should be treated. Cases with a tourniquet in position demand the first attention; those known or suspected to have sustained fractures of the limbs should follow; then cases with injuries of the head, and finally those with flesh wounds. Cases of penetrating wounds of the abdomen may well be left until the end, as they will require more time and equipment; should they, in fact, have died in the hour or two before their turn comes for operation, earlier treatment would probably not have avoided the fatal issue. Patients with burns require no further attention until such time as the effect of their first dose of morphia is passing off, when the question of repeating the dose will arise.

---

* The danger of patients smoking while under morphia and burning themselves and their blankets must be borne in mind.

The following treatment is suggested for the various types of cases mentioned above.

(1) *Patients still having a tourniquet about a limb.*

These will fall into two classes, those whose hæmorrhage, although initially alarming, did not really necessitate this extreme measure, and those with such severe arterial bleeding that the application of a tourniquet was a life-saving measure.

In either case the tourniquet should not be loosened until (*a*) the whole wound or wounds are exposed by removing any temporary dressing and a sufficiency of clothing, (*b*) until the surgeon has an assistant at his side, and (*c*) until artery forceps, some ligature material, ample dressings and bandages are at hand. Inspection of the wound may decide that its position renders damage to a large artery impossible; in such a case when the tourniquet is removed there may be very little bleeding, and the opportunity is taken to remove from the wound obvious foreign bodies, whether metal or pieces of clothing. An adequate dressing of flavine gauze is then applied.

Inspection of the wound may indicate that a large vessel has probably been damaged; in these cases the wisest course is to clear the wound of any clot, clothing or other foreign body; the edges should next be held apart and only then should the assistant be instructed to loosen slowly the tourniquet. If it prove impossible to secure quickly with artery forceps the arterial bleeding (which is almost certain to occur) the tourniquet must be re-tightened,

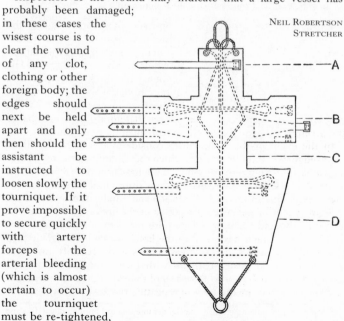

NEIL ROBERTSON
STRETCHER

A

B

C

D

and the wound again cleared of blood; the procedure being repeated until the bleeding has been successfully controlled. The artery forceps are then left *in situ*, until a decision is reached as to what further treatment of the case is required; treatment is not completed until satisfactory ligatures have replaced the artery forceps.

Only if uncertainty is felt regarding the complete arrest of arterial hæmorrhage should a tourniquet be left loosely on the limb, and *it is most important that the Medical Officer satisfies himself that the tourniquet is really loose*. When possible a pencil mark over the femoral, subclavian or brachial artery should be made so that an assistant can re-apply pressure should bleeding recur in transit.

It should be remembered that removal of a tourniquet from the thigh may easily lead to a fall in blood pressure so that a careful watch must be kept on the patient and the limb elevated.

(2) *Cases with fractures of the limbs.*—The treatment of such cases is fully described in Part III. In a small ship improvised splints may well have to take the place of standard patterns; every splint applied should be comfortable, padded and so adjusted as to render unlikely the need for any re-adjustment until after the case is evacuated.

First Aid Treatment for Compound Fractures:—

    (1) Give a full dose of morphia.

    (2) Immobilise the limb temporarily upon a splint even if in a deformed or displaced position.

    (3) Any attempt at manipulation or reduction should be avoided.

    (4) Do not wash the skin or irrigate the wound, as this may carry infection into the wound.

    (5) Lightly dust the area with sulphanilamide powder and apply a sterile dressing.

(3) *Injuries to the head.*—First-aid in such cases is confined to dressing any associated wound of the scalp and should be preceded by shaving a good area of scalp around. The wound should be dusted with sulphanilamide powder. As a rule the application of a dressing is sufficient to arrest bleeding; if not, the edges of the scalp wound may be approximated by a few sutures tied over the dressing. Restlessness in an unconscious patient is controlled by small, i.e., gr. one-twelfth doses of morphia, and the unconscious man should be placed in such a position, usually on his side, as will reduce the chance of his choking during unconsciousness.

Further details of the treatment in this class of case are given in Part III, much of which cannot be carried out, however, in any but the larger type of fighting ship.

(4) The majority of the remaining casualties will fall into the class of *flesh wounds*. In these cases the first dressing should be removed and the wound very gently explored with the finger or a clean narrow instrument. Any accessible foreign bodies revealed should be removed; dead tags of skin or protruding fascia or muscle must be cut away; any reactionary bleeding is arrested and a flavine gauze dressing applied. If extensive flesh wounds are present or if the wound is anywhere near a joint splinting will promote the patient's comfort.

Three more general matters call for notice:—

(*a*) By the time this early treatment of the cases has been completed many may require a second dose of morphia.

(*b*) In patients unconscious after head injuries or paralysed below the waist from injuries to the spinal cord, the necessity of preventing over-distension of the bladder must not be overlooked.

(*c*) In other injuries in the neighbourhood of the pelvis retention of urine may also occur. If clinical examination reveals a full bladder, a catheter must be passed. In view of the disaster that may follow infection of the urinary tract, especially in the first two groups of cases, it is the duty of the medical officer to pass the catheter himself, with all due precautions against infection.

Guidance as to how best to proceed in cases in which retention recurs or persists will be found in Part III, page 23.

(5) *Amputations.*—There is only one occasion in which the Medical Officer of a small ship may find himself confronted with the necessity of performing an immediate amputation as a First Aid measure, namely, when such an operation is required to liberate a casualty pinned by a heavy object.

After giving a full dose of morphia and, if possible, under an anaesthetic, a tourniquet should be applied and the limb severed by knife and saw at the site of injury. After application of dressing and splint the patient is moved to a suitable place in which to complete the operation (*see* Part III).

Other indications for amputation are described in Part III.

Some notes on the treatment of *ophthalmic injuries* and *perforated ear-drums* are included in Part III

Intravenous Therapy. The indications for intravenous therapy and the full technique are described in B.R. 110 and B.R. 22.

Sets of Dried Blood Serum and apparatus for administration are now available for ships carrying a medical officer and should be demanded in accordance with A.F.O. 4671/41 and A.F.O. 74/42.

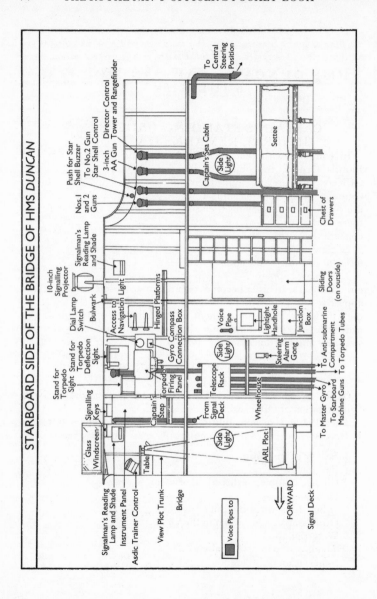

STARBOARD SIDE OF THE BRIDGE OF HMS *DUNCAN*

To Central Steering Position

Push for Star Shell Buzzer

Director Control Tower and Rangefinder

3-inch AA Gun Control

To No.2 Gun Star Shell Control

Nos.1 and 2 Guns

Captain's Sea Cabin

Settee

Chest of Drawers

Signalman's Reading Lamp and Shade

10-inch Signalling Projector

Dial Lamp Switch

Access to Navigation Light

Bulwark

Hinged Platforms

Side Light

Voice Pipe

Sliding Doors (on outside)

Lighthit Handhole

Junction Box

Stand for Torpedo Sight

Stand for Torpedo Deflection Sight

Gyro Compass Connection Box

Torpedo Firing Panel

Steering Alarm Gong

Side Light

To Anti-submarine Compartment

To Torpedo Tubes

Signalling Keys

Captain's Step

From Signal Deck

Telescope Rack

Wheelhouse

Glass Windscreen

Table

Side Light

ARL Plot

To Master Gyro

To Starboard Machine Guns

Signalman's Reading Lamp and Shade

Instrument Panel

Asdic Trainer Control

View Plot Trunk

Bridge

FORWARD

Signal Deck

Voice Pipes to

CHAPTER IV
HMS DUNCAN – CAPTAIN'S ORDERS
6 JULY 1943

CAPTAIN'S STANDING ORDERS No.1
GENERAL REMARKS ON ORDERS

In common with that of K.R. & A.I. and various Fleet and Flotilla Orders, the object of the following orders is to assist Officers in carrying out their duties efficiently and along common lines. To this end, I would impress upon all Officers the importance of making themselves thoroughly acquainted with these and with any of the above orders and instructions which concern them.

2. Similarly, the Ship's Orders are designed to assist in the efficient running of the ship.

3. It may happen that as a result of experience, or change of circumstances, an order becomes redundant, or obsolete. Should this appear to any Officer to be the case, he should report the matter to me with a view to the amendment, or cancellation, of that order. An order which is in existence but which is not enforced, is a germ of slackness and inefficiency.

CAPTAIN'S STANDING ORDERS No.2
OFFICER OF THE DAY IN HARBOUR

(K.R. & A.I. Articles 1152, 660 and 178). See also No.8 'Investigation of Offences'.

The O.O.D.'s responsibilities are indicated in general terms in K.R. & A.I. (see above). Some points of detail are given below.

2. Safety of the Ship.
    Barometer,
    Change in force, or direction, of wind,
    Dragging,
    Other ships dragging foul of us,
    Other ships under weigh in the vicinity,
    Watertight doors,
    Tending of wires when alongside,
    Supervision of 'welders'.

3. Boats.
Coming alongside,
Away under sail,
Motorboats broken
     down,
Safe load
     appropriate to
     weather,
Lifebelts,
Moored up,
Appearance.

4. Routine and
Orderly Conduct.
Meal hours,
Rounds,
Libertymen,
Unoccupied compartments,
Smoking,
Dress,
Ventilation,
Colours and Sunset,
Tidiness generally,
Supervision of sentries.
Security.

5. Reports to Commanding Officer.
The O.O.D. is to inform me, or in my absence the
Commanding Officer,
(a) If the weather becomes threatening, if the barometer starts
to fall rapidly, or if there is any sudden change in the wind.
(b) If there seems to be any danger of the ship being fouled by
another ship.
(c) If in doubt at any time.
Note. I am always accessible, whether awake, or sleeping—See
also No. 4., 'O.O.W. at Sea', para. 1.

CAPTAIN'S STANDING ORDERS No.3
ANCHOR WATCH
Anchor Watch is always to be kept when at anchor.
2.   The O.O.W. is responsible that
(a) Steam is on the Capstan Engine and that the Engineer

Officer is informed that this is required—if I require it.

(b) Another anchor is ready to let go.

(c) A leadsman is near the chains, with lead on the bottom.

(d) Anchor bearings are taken and entered in the log.

(e) The Commanding Officer is informed at the least sign of dragging.

(f) That the cable is ready for instant slipping.

3. The Engineer Officer is to obtain orders regarding Main Engines from the Commanding Officer.

CAPTAIN'S STANDING ORDERS No.4
OFFICER OF THE WATCH—AT SEA
(K.R. & A.I. Article 1152, 1160, 1187).

Calling The Captain.

After a period of constant wakefulness, or disturbed rest, a man is sometimes capable of making an apparently intelligent reply, when called, without really waking up. *Whenever I am called by the O.O.W. it is my intention to come on to the bridge* unless I consider the cause of the call not to be of immediate importance, in which event I shall say so. I rely upon the O.O.W. to assist me in carrying out this intention, and any reluctance on his part to disturb me, however well meant, will be misplaced.

Safety of The Ship.

2. The Officer of the Watch is responsible for the safety of the ship. He is *NOT* relieved of this responsibility by the presence on the Bridge of a Senior Officer.

3. He is never to hesitate to call me at any time if in doubt or difficulty. He has full authority, however, to take such action as he considers necessary for the safety of the ship without waiting for my approval.

4. He is constantly to bear in mind his responsibility for the ship as a whole. For example, should the weather conditions seem to be deteriorating, or should the ship be about to alter to a course which will increase the rolling, he is to take such action as may be necessary for additional battening down and securing of gear.

Emergencies.

5. He is constantly to bear in mind what immediate action to take in the event of sudden emergencies, such as:—

(a) Sighting an enemy surface vessel, submarine or aircraft. Asdic or R.D.F. contact with a submarine. Note 1:—See new C.B. 4097. Note 2:—In my absence the O.O.W. is responsible for giving the order to 'open fire'.

(b) The torpedoing of a ship in the convoy, or any behaviour out of the ordinary.

(c) Man overboard from his own ship or from the next ahead.

Compasses.

6. The sperry repeater is to be checked by azimuth, or shore bearings, before leaving harbour and, when practicable, on every alteration of course. It is also to be checked with the magnetic compass every hour and on alteration of course, and the result is to be entered in the log.

Reports.

7. The following reports are always to be made to me:—

(a) The sighting of all ships, lights or land.

(b) Any material change in visibility or weather conditions.

(c) If any vessel appears likely to pass within a mile of the ship or of any vessel in company.

Note:—If it is necessary to alter course in accordance with the Rule of the Road, the O.O.W. is to act in plenty of time and in such a manner as to leave no doubt in the other ship as to his intentions.

(d) If the ship gets badly out of station.

(e) All alterations of course or speed, except small alterations necessary for station keeping.

(f) Any wreckage, or unusual behaviour on the part of any ship or vessel.

(g) Sunset and that navigation lights and V/F gear are correct.

8. The O.O.W. must remember that he is the S.O. Escort's representative, as well as the representative of 'Duncan'. I therefore wish to know at once anything which might affect the convoy or its escort, e.g., aircraft in sight, escorts out of station, stragglers. Always report if in doubt. I have little to do at sea, except when in contact with the 'wolfpacks'.

CAPTAIN'S STANDING ORDERS No.5
MANOEUVRING MAIN ENGINES

The term 'Abandon Ship' is *never* to be used. In any emergency 'Crash Stations' will be piped or sounded on Alarm Rattlers, and formost messdecks are cleared as quickly as possible, last man in each space shutting the watertight door.

2. The 'Crash Stations' allocation for lifesaving is not to include the boats, which can seldom be got out in an emergency. Signal— succession of Shorts on Alarm Rattlers. The Watch 'on' remain at their posts.

3. The orders on the Engine Room Telegraphs are to be obeyed as follows:—

SLOW ahead or astern —40 revs. per minute.

HALF ahead —100 revs. per minute, or as ordered by the revolution telegraph.

HALF astern —100 revs. per minute, or as ordered by telegraph.

FULL ahead or astern —Maximum speed available with the number of boilers alight.

Notes:—(1) 'FULL' speed will only be used in an *Emergency*. Normally telegraphs will be kept at 'HALF' and speed altered by the revolution telegraph if more than 40 revs. are required.

(2) The telegraphs are *not* to be obeyed in harbour, when getting under weigh, until the order 'Obey Engine Room Telegraphs' has been passed by telephone from the Bridge.

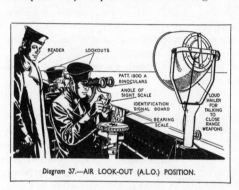 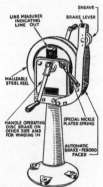

Diagram 37.—AIR LOOK-OUT (A.L.O.) POSITION.

CAPTAIN'S STANDING ORDERS No.6
STEERING GEAR—BREAKDOWN

Should the steering gear break down, the main object will be to get the ship under control again as soon as possible. The first step will therefore be to shift to 'Steer by Main Engines' and to con the ship from the bridge through the direct telephone to the Engine Room, and by telegraphs.

2. Subsequently, when clear of danger from grounding or collision, it may be more convenient to shift from 'Steer by Main Engines' steering to the After Steering position, where there is a compass. It may be necessary to steer from Tiller Flat.

Procedure.

3. O.O.W. notices, or Q.M. reports—Steering gear broken down, or wheel jammed.

4. O.O.W. informs Engine Room—'Steering gear broken down, steer by Main Engines'

5. Q.M. puts the wheel amidships if possible and locks it.

6. O.O.W. cons the ship through the direct telephone to the Engine Room, and by telegraphs. Engineer Officer then investigates and reports the quickest method of centring the rudder.

Should E.R. Telephone Break Down.

7. O.O.W. stations a hand by the after E.R. Hatch to pass down wheel orders received by semaphore from the Bridge as follows (as seen from *AFT*):—

'Port 10'	'Port 20'	'Amidships'
'Starboard 10'	'Starboard 20'	

Waved round and round . . . . . . 'Steady'.

Steering by Main Engines.

8. As soon as the ship has been got under control with the main engines the telegraphs will be put to 'Half Speed Ahead Together' and the order passed to steer by Main Engines. Revolutions for the one engine will then be ordered by telephone and those for the other engine by the revolution telegraph.

Engine Room Telegraph—Breakdown.

9. Should the telegraphs break down orders will be passed by the direct telephone to the Engine Room or, if that fails, by telephone to the Depthcharge Sentry and thence by voicepipe to the Engine Room. If the latter becomes necessary and the repair of the bridge telegraphs will be lengthy, the after steering position telegraphs will be manned and connected up.

Procedure.

10. O.O.W. informs Engine Room—'Bridge telegraphs broken down. Orders for Main Engines will be passed by telephone (or by voicepipe from After steering position).'

CAPTAIN'S STANDING ORDERS No.6A
BREAKDOWN OF ENGINES

If, through failure of lubrication or any other cause, it is necessary to stop the engines suddenly, the Engine Room should ring a succession of rings on the Engine Room Reply Gongs, and then report by telephone.

CAPTAIN'S STANDING ORDERS No.7
DELEGATED AUTHORITY TO PUNISH

In accordance with K.R. & A.I. Article 536, authority to award the following punishments is hereby delegated to:—

(a) The Executive Officer, if a Lieutenant.
   No. 11 for Seven Days,
   No. 12 for Fourteen Days, but not to apply to Petty Officers,
   No. 16 to the full extent.
(b) The Engineer Officer,
   No. 16 to the full extent.
(c) The Officer of the Day, if a Lieutenant,
   No. 16 for One Day.

CAPTAIN'S STANDING ORDERS No.8
INVESTIGATION OF OFFENCES

(K.R. & A.I. Article 537).

No avoidable delay is to take place in the investigation into offences or complaints: such delay wastes the time of the complainants, the witnesses and the accused, and discourages Petty Officers and Leading Rates in the execution of this part of their duties.

2. All alleged offences are to be investigated fully in the first instance. It is important that all evidence should be taken before witnesses have time to discuss the matter with each other.

3. Serious offences and all charges of drunkenness against persons of and above Leading Rate are to be investigated by the First Lieutenant, if on board.

4. Care is to be taken that the correct caution is given to any man about to make a statement, as specified in K.R. & A.I. 537 (6). A summary of the evidence of all witnesses is to be taken down in writing and, if any statement is made by the accused, it is to be taken down carefully in his own words, read over to him and signed by him and by the investigating officer.

5. **Refusal of Duty.** If a rating is brought up for 'Refusal of Duty' he is to be told that such an offence is one of the most serious against discipline. Further, that if after five minutes consideration, he thinks better of it and obeys the order, he will only be charged with 'Not immediately obeying the order', the result of which will probably not affect his future career as would the offence of refusal of duty.

6. If he still persists, the offender is to be placed under arrest by order of the Executive Officer.

7. Care is to be taken not to aggravate the offence by repeating the order.

8. **Placing under arrest.** Except in cases of violence involving the necessity of immediate restraint, no person is to be put under arrest unless such action is ordered by the Executive Officer.

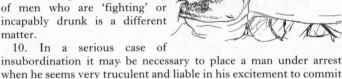

9. The safeguarding in custody of men who are 'fighting' or incapably drunk is a different matter.

10. In a serious case of insubordination it may be necessary to place a man under arrest when he seems very truculent and liable in his excitement to commit himself still further.

11. Care should be taken that a drunken or excited man is not given an opportunity to aggravate his offence, e.g., by striking.

12. **Drunkenness.** It is the responsibility of the officer investigating the charge to decide whether or not the accused is drunk, as defined by K.R. & A.I. Article 462A: but, if there is reasonable doubt whether a man owes his condition to drink or to illness, or if there is reason to suppose that he has drunk such a quantity as to make medical attention necessary, or should he request to see a doctor, he should be sent to the Sick Bay under escort for examination by the Medical Officer.

13. In the absence of the Medical Officer, the Medical Officer of the Guard should be sent for at the discretion of the Officer of the Day.

14. In cases of drunkenness, however, where there is a possibility of the accused being tried by Court Martial (i.e. where Petty Officers or persons of higher rank are concerned), a Medical Officer should always be sent for.

15. The purpose of the Medical Officer's examination is NOT to decide whether the accused is 'drunk' in the service sense of the word, but to discover whether his condition is due to sickness or liquor.

16. **Striking and offences of violence.** It is desirable that the accused should be examined by the Medical Officer as soon as possible after the commission of the offence, so as to discover his mental and physical condition at the time.

17. Where there are no witnesses to a striking case it is important that both the accused and the victim should be examined by the

Medical Officer in order to corroborate the statement of the victim by medical evidence of the probability of any injuries having been caused by the accused striking the victim.

18. **Unnatural offences.** All officers should make themselves familiar with C.A.F.O. 1955/29 (amended by C.A.F.O. 648/40), which gives full instructions for dealing with investigations of charges under this heading.

CAPTAIN'S STANDING ORDERS No.9
ISSUE OF RUM

The Gunner is to superintend the getting up and issue of Rum daily. Any shortage, when pumping up a cask or otherwise, is to be reported to the Executive Officer.

2. In the absence of the Gunner, this duty is to be carried out by the Officer of the Day.

CAPTAIN'S STANDING ORDERS No.10
OFFICERS' LEAVE

Officers are free to go ashore out of working hours when not required for duty.

2. Officers wishing to sleep ashore are to obtain my permission and are responsible that adequate arrangements are made for their recall in emergency.

CAPTAIN'S STANDING ORDERS No.11
OFFICERS' MESS & WINE BILLS
(K.R. & A.I. Articles 619, 621 and 1138).

Officers are to settle their Mess Bills as soon as practicable after the end of the month. The First Lieutenant is to report to me on the 10th of the month the name of any Officer who has not settled his previous month's mess bill.

2. Officers are not to borrow money from the Ward Room Steward or from Mess Funds, nor are they to require the Steward to settle other than small shore accounts on their behalf.

3. The regulations regarding Wine Bills are given in K.R. & A.I. Article 619.

CAPTAIN'S STANDING ORDERS No.11A
CARE OF NON-PUBLIC FUNDS

The following non-public funds are authorised to be on board:—

Fund.	Secretary & Treasurer.
Ship's Fund (including Tombola)	First Lieutenant.
W.R. Mess Fund	Sub. Lieut. Roberts—
	Caterer—Mr. Foster.
W.R. Wine Fund & Mineral Fund	Surgeon-Lieut. Campbell
W.R. Tobacco Fund Sub. Lieut. Cowlin.	

2. The First Lieutenant is to supervise generally all non-public funds.

3. The Officer in charge of each fund is to keep proper accounts. Attention is drawn to K.R. & A.I. Article 635, para. 3.

4. Audits are to be carried out in accordance with K.R. & A.I. Article 635A, on February 28th, June 30th, November 30th, and on change of secretaries. Completed forms S.256 are to be submitted to me by 5th March, July and November. L.G.O. 260 refers.

Auditing Officers will be detailed by First Lieutenant.

5. The attention of Officers keeping accounts is directed to K.R. & A.I. Articles 619, 621, 623 and 635A.

6. No non-public funds other than those mentioned are to be opened without my written approval.

CAPTAIN'S STANDING ORDERS No.12
CUSTODY OF CONFIDENTIAL
BOOKS & PUBLICATIONS

The attention of all officers who have C.B.s or any other confidential publications on their charge, is drawn to the instructions contained in C.B. U2.D.

2. The Signal Officer, as C.B. Officer, is to be in charge of C.B.s, S.P.s, and all confidential matter, which has to be taken on charge.

3. On receipt on board, all confidential books and Signal Publications are to be handed direct to the C.B. Officer, who is responsible that they are shown to the Captain and the Executive Officer, and that those which relate to their departments or duties are shown to the Officers concerned.

4. The C.B. Officer is responsible for the correction of all C.B.s and S.P.s on charge, except when they are issued on loan to individual Officers, who then become responsible for making the necessary corrections. The C.B. Officer, however, is responsible that Officers not in receipt of C.A.F.O. 'S' series are informed of the receipt of any corrections to the C.B.s on loan to them.

5. Corrections are to be made without delay on receipt of the addenda or A.F.O. authorising them. The insertion of all corrections is to be noted on the inside of the front cover of the book, or on the appropriate certificate provided in certain books.

CAPTAIN'S STANDING ORDERS No.15
INSPECTION OF BOOKS

Books will be inspected weekly on Wednesdays, and monthly on the first Thursday in the month.

2. The following books are to be in my Cabin by 10.00 on Wednesdays, completed to the preceding Saturday:—

3. The following books are to be in my Cabin by 10.00 on the first Thursday of every month:—

Wine Books,
Gangway Wine Book,
Daily Record,
Minor Punishments Book,
Registered Letter and Parcel Book,
Ship's Log,
Magazine Log,
Engine Room Register,
Night Rounds Book,
Defect Books,
Signal and W/T Logs,
Cypher Logs,
Daily Issue Book,
Spirit Stoppage Book.

Torpedo Work Book,
Gunnery Log,
Provision Account,
Loan Clothing Account,
Postage Account Book,
Gyro Compass Log,
Asdic and Hydrophone Journal,
Railway Warrant Book,
Store Accounts,
Navigational Data Book,
R.D.F. Log,
Implement Account—Cox'n
    do. do. —W.R.
A. and A. Book,
Double Bottoms Books
Daily Sick Book.

CAPTAIN'S STANDING ORDERS No.16
CORRESPONDENCE

All official correspondence is to pass through my office. Correspondence marked 'Immediate', 'Important' or 'Receipt to be acknowledged' and telegrams addressed to the Commanding Officer are to be delivered personally to the Correspondence Officer, or, if he is not on board, to the Officer of the Day.

2. In my absence such correspondence is to be dealt with by the Commanding Officer.

CAPTAIN'S STANDING ORDERS No.17
SIGNALS

No signal is to be made from the ship without my authority.

2. If I am out of the ship and an immediate action is required, the Senior Officer on board is to make the necessary signals. Otherwise, wait until I return.

CAPTAIN'S STANDING ORDERS No.18
SMARTNESS

The tendency for small ships during this War is to grow steadily more slack in points like dress, appearance of ship, cleanliness and general smartness.

2. There is no need for this and I would like all Officers to help in preserving a high standard.

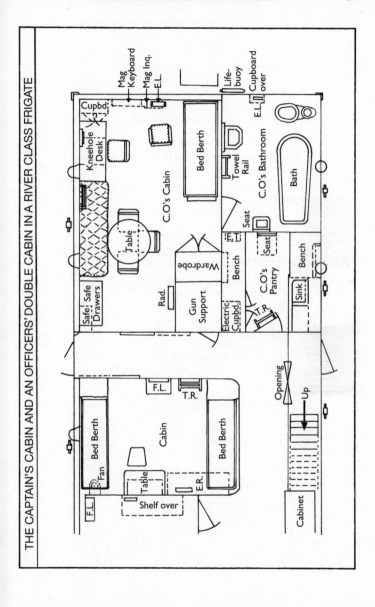

THE CAPTAIN'S CABIN AND AN OFFICERS' DOUBLE CABIN IN A RIVER CLASS FRIGATE

CHAPTER V
YOUR SHIP
Notes and Advice to An Officer on Assuming His First Command
1944

FOREWORD BY SECOND SEA LORD

This booklet contains accumulated experience on a number of matters bearing on the art of Command.

I have had it produced believing that it will meet a need in helping officers on first assuming command of one of H.M. Ships.

I hope it may also be useful to the thousands of officers of the Royal Navy, Royal Naval Reserve and Royal Naval Volunteer Reserve already in command, especially those to whom the war has brought this distinction and responsibility at a comparatively early age.

A. W. WILLIS,
Admiral.

1: YOURSELF
THE AIM

The assumption of your first command is the greatest step that you will ever take. It carries with it not only the responsibility of a King's ship, but the power to mould or mar the characters of a large body of men. It carries with it an historic tradition of dignity and privilege, and in return it makes demands on your skill and endurance, which have never before been asked, and which brook no failure.

This book takes for granted that you have the necessary attributes of leadership and knowledge to assume that command. It tries to make your first six months easier by giving you a mould into which to pour those attributes—a mould fashioned in the foundry of many distinguished Commanding Officers.

THE COMMAND OUTLOOK

If you have been a First Lieutenant you have already mastered the organisation of a ship; you have a good knowledge of Armament Control; you have a great pride in the appearance of your ship; and you have a general knowledge on matters concerning personnel. If you have been a specialist your flair for organisation has been more localised, but in both cases your work has been to a certain extent departmental.

What do you as a Commanding Officer require over and above this outlook?

Firstly, you require to realise that, once appointed in command, no matter what rank you hold, you are The Captain, which means that you are the ship—that when a fender is left over the side it is *your* fender left over by *your* O.O.D., that when a confidential document is mislaid by a Sub-Lieutenant it is still *your* document, that when a seaman from your crew is seen wearing his cap flat-aback ashore, that seaman is reflecting a lack of pride in *your* ship; and that when you hit the tug and not the target with your first salvo it is *your* deflection that is wrong.

Secondly, you require an increased consciousness of your Personal Example. Few Officers on assuming command realise to what extent their personality is mirrored in the ship. Every word which you say on the bridge is noted by the ship's company. Every word you say in the wardroom is marked by the Officers. A display of unwarranted temper on the bridge, an unjust or over-hasty reprimand, a careless piece of shiphandling, an uncloaked show of anxiety, all these incidents will be reflected by your Officers and men just as the planets reflect the light of the sun. Similarly, a disregard of danger on the bridge carries courage to every corner of the ship.

Your example in the wardroom will be followed. A Captain who holds up meals for a considerable time and thereby wastes his Officers' and his stewards' time, must expect an equal lack of consideration elsewhere. A Captain who is a consistently heavy drinker automatically encourages high wine bills. The competence of those Officers whose heads are not as strong as his will be reduced.

Thirdly, as Commanding Officer you should exercise a different type of authority to that used by a Head of Department. It might best be called the 'managerial' authority. Whereas a First Lieutenant, or

Specialist, orders and administers, a Captain supervises and directs. It is of course obvious that a few definite Standing Orders concerning the administration of a ship must be issued, but too many of these orders fetter the flexibility of good administration, and, worse still, a percentage of them slip into abeyance and often come to be disregarded, with a consequent bad effect on discipline. Similarly, if you are constantly sending for your Officers and ordering them to take this or that precaution, or to carry out this or that improvement, and if you issue voluminous night orders, your Officers come to depend upon you to think out all eventualities rather than themselves.

Fourthly, a Captain's outlook must embrace the flotilla or unit as well as his own particular ship. As a First Lieutenant or Staff Officer your attitude to the rest of your unit was naturally competitive. It was your pride to have the cleanest ship. You wished to carry off every trophy at sports, and to win any armament and signal competition going. Once again, as a Captain it is necessary to take a broader view.

The flotilla or squadron must act completely as a unit. Your loyalty to your ship should work in unison with your flotilla loyalty, and never in antipathy. Some Commanding Officers, forgetful of this maxim, will allow a number of leave privileges or engineer a mail speed-up for their own ship, quite regardless of the considerable damage it will do in the other ships, whose crews soon hear of it and will think that their own Officers are letting them down.

By all means have the smartest ship in the unit, but do so by fair means, and, when it comes to benefits bestowed, see that they are bestowed on all the unit and not only on your own ship. In war time you will often find yourself in harbour with a mixed crowd of ships, and often you may find yourself Senior Officer of a group. Here the same thing applies. They may not be your own flotilla, but any 'wangles' you arrange must be dealt out in equal portions.

Another new relationship will be that of the flotilla or

squadron staff. There is often a tendency in the wardroom to make light of the staff, and to pass innumerable remarks about the time spent in harbour by the leader or flagship. This is a childish outlook. The best ship will be in complete harmony with the staff, and the best Captain will be the one who enjoys mutual confidence with the staff. Without this attitude there can be no flotilla team-work or spirit.

The final essential outlook can best be summed up by referring to an old expression, which has been nearly submerged in the hum of modern machinery. It was not so long ago that Captains referred to their ship's company as 'My People.' Whether you use that expression or not is immaterial: it is the feeling behind it that matters.

As Captain you have definite moral and paternal obligations to your ship's company. They look to you for absolute justice on board. They seek your advice and help in their family difficulties ashore.

As Captain, too, you have definite religious obligations, which are carefully laid down in the King's Regulations and Admiralty Instructions. It is up to you to keep services above the level of parade ritual, and to see that all denominations have every chance to attend their separate churches.

Thus it can be seen that a broader outlook in every respect is required of an officer who assumes command.

THE PITFALLS

Having shown, then, that a change to a broader outlook is necessary on assuming command, it is worth while mentioning the pitfalls, which some of your predecessors have fallen into, in the hopes that you will be able to avoid them.

The first temptation comes with the 'take over' itself. This is the inclination to be entirely overwhelmed by the secretarial side of your duties to the detriment of the fighting and personnel side. In order to cope with the maintenance and correction of some hundreds of secret and confidential books and documents whose loss might seriously affect your career, and in order to conduct the correspondence of your ship you must, unless you carry a Paymaster, rely on young Sub-Lieutenants with no secretarial training, and plenty of other duties, who work in an office which no business man would tolerate. The resultant anxiety will naturally be great, and you must needs give plenty of initial supervision to your amateur secretaries. At the same time your first and foremost duty is to fight your ship, and you must keep a balanced sense of proportion in this respect. There will be plenty among your files of text books, orders, memoranda, tactical data, etc., to absorb, before you can give full attention to the lesser aspects of the secretariat. And even these books should not keep you from acquiring an immediate knowledge of your ship and ship's company. In the hectic first weeks do not remain shut in your cabin surrounded by order books.

Another temptation concerning correspondence must be dealt with by equal self-firmness. This is an early tendency to burst into official letterpress at the slightest provocation. It is due to an early excess of self-assertiveness, but it can be very aggravating to your unit staff and Senior Officers. A number of young C.O.s imagine that the high road to promotion is paved with daily letters commencing 'The following suggestion. . . is submitted.' In nine cases out of ten all the ideas that you think of in your first six months have been tried before you joined. If, therefore, you have any inspiration for the better prosecution of war, or the increased efficiency of your unit, it is worth while finding out verbally from the staff whether the idea is acceptable, or merely a discarded 'annual,' before you send it in as a letter.

Having stressed the danger of paying disproportionate attention to paperwork at the beginning of your command, it is now the moment to point out the dangers of neglecting the 'written word.'

It is so very easy in warfare to succumb to the heroic vision of being a fighter and not a writer that some Captains neither produce concise orders, nor bother about their execution. At all times, but especially in wartime, the Captain must devote consistent supervision to the disciplinary side of administration, which is normally embodied in his Standing Orders.

Experience of the Fleet has shown that a large number of serious offences could have been avoided if the Captain's Standing Orders, particularly those concerning rum, and the inspection of libertymen returning from leave, had been more concisely written, and more rigidly applied.

The supply and issue of rum needs a Commanding Officer's keenest supervision.

It is essential that an Officer attends daily issue, and checks most carefully the supply and opening of new casks. Supply Ratings will only fall to the temptation of misappropriation or the falsifying of accounts if they know that the Officers are out of touch with the situation.

The prevention of serious cases due to libertymen under the influence of drink or men in an excited condition being allowed to commit themselves further needs not only concise orders but definite instruction to your duty officers. Cases occur when libertymen return onboard under the influence of drink, and either because they are not inspected at all, or because of a misapplied leniency on the part of the O.O.D. they are allowed to go forward, where, having lost the mastery of their respect and reason due to drink, they commit some crime such as striking or insubordination, which they would not have done under normal circumstances. For this reason your orders should lay down that all libertymen returning onboard are to be inspected by the O.O.D., and you must impress on all Duty Officers that a man returning onboard under the influence of drink should be put under sentry's charge primarily in his own interests and the interests of his messmates.

In the same connection, if a man is brought before the O.O.D. when in a highly excited condition, consideration must be given to putting him below in preventive custody. If he is placed in the First Lieutenant's report and told to carry on, he may well aggravate his offence due to a sense of aggrievement and to his state of excitement.

Another pitfall of your early days in command is to live in the past and not in the present. If you have been a First Lieutenant there is an inclination to 'revert to type' and interfere in your own First Lieutenant's job. He will appreciate your advice on small matters of internal administration, but he will resent detailed instructions. If you have specialised there is a temptation to range over the ground familiar to you rather than to cover your whole demesne with a balanced eye. Maybe it enhances your confidence, but it will destroy the confidence of other people.

Another way of 'reverting to type' is to become too much of a Wardroom Officer. In the smallest ships the Captain is inevitably a member of the mess and its president, but in ships like a destroyer he is an honorary member, and has a comfortable day cabin of his own in which to sit. He should normally have lunch and dinner in the wardroom as this will help him to know his Officers, but his continued presence is bound to have somewhat restricting influence, as is exemplified by the tradition that the Officers should stand when the Captain comes into the mess. A Captain should therefore not outstay his welcome.

But not all the pitfalls are in the first lap. Although handling your ship may cause you most anxiety for the first few months, the most dangerous period for the new Captain is round about the sixth. All the months before this you have been improving steadily, until you have finally become in your own mind the traditionally brilliant and dashing small-ship Captain. Your ship responds to your 'aids' like a polo pony. The forethought you originally put into going alongside no longer appears necessary. A touch astern will remedy any early misjudgment. Then the crash comes. The ship's company may appreciate your period in dock, but the Commander-in-Chief will not.

The final and most important temptation which confronts every Commanding Officer is the same as that which has brought so many dictators to the ground. 'Power corrupts' is a dictum which does not only apply to politics. Bernard Shaw has recently enlarged on this by stating 'Power corrupts the weak and dements the strong.' As a Commanding Officer you are an autocrat pure and simple, and you are subject to the same temptations as an autocrat. No one in your ship can check your excesses, or point out your eccentricities; no one can question your more downright assertions; everyone must endure your temper or any other foible you may develop. You are treated with the deference and ceremony not always granted to a cabinet minister.

All this has the effect of accentuating your weaknesses, unless you watch yourself most carefully. Only some candid and regular introspection will keep you in command of yourself. The forces which turned Captain Bligh into a tyrant, though perhaps weaker, are still extant. Bligh was in many ways a good character; he was an efficient Officer and a competent seaman; he possessed great courage and powers of endurance; but he had insufficient strength of will to repress two instincts, which are normally repressed in youth. He submitted himself to unbridled temper, and to sadism. The modern laws of the Navy rightly do not tolerate a practical application of the latter, but do not forget that it is within your power to cause considerable mental anguish to your younger officers by a consistent tone of sarcasm and contempt, and that, after the undue strain and fatigue of command in warfare, it is quite as simple to submit to such childish teasing instincts as it is to give way to undignified temper and intolerance over small and petty irritations. And what is worse, *nobody* is going to tell you about them. In all Officers, but above all in Commanding Officers, the words Officer and Gentleman should be entirely synonymous.

THE FRAMEWORK OF DISCIPLINE

Having read earlier in this chapter of the 'managerial' outlook required of a Commanding Officer, many Officers will find it difficult to fuse so loose a word into the rigid framework of service discipline.

It is agreed that there must be a most definite understanding between you and your Officers on the observance of your authority, and it is suggested that you clarify this degree of observance required by giving your Officers three grades of orders as enumerated below, and by sticking rigidly to them yourself.

The Grade of Order	The written example	The spoken example	The Observance
(1) The Imperative	The Captain's Standing Orders	Do this! Repaint the whaler to-day,	Immediate execution
(2) The volitive	Instructions to O.O.D's in harbour, etc.	I wish you to do this! I want the whaler repainted at the first opportunity	Execution unless there appears reason not to, in which case representation to C.O.
(3) The Admonitive	Captain's Memos. Notes on the use of . . . . . . Aide Memoire on . . . . Advice on	I suggest you do this. . . . Isn't it time the whaler had a fresh coat, Number One?	Voluntary execution, disregard of which may be a little tactless.

CONCLUSION

This chapter has shown you how your outlook must broaden on assuming command; it has also shown you some of the pitfalls of command. It has made no attempt to define the perfect Captain, for such an attempt would entail a long catalogue of abstract qualities, which have never yet been invested in one man.

In conclusion, however, and in introduction to the next chapters, it reproduces an extract from a letter written by Paul Jones to the Naval Committee of Congress in 1775, on which every Commanding Officer to-day could well base his conduct.

'Coming now to view the Naval Officer aboard ship and in relation to those under his command, he should be the soul of tact, patience, justice, firmness and charity. No meritorious act of a subordinate should escape his attention or be left to pass without its reward, if even the reward be only one word of approval. Conversely, he should not be blind to a single fault in any subordinate, though at the same time he should be quick and unfailing to distinguish error from malice, thoughtlessness from incompetency, and well-meaning short-coming from heedless or stupid blunder. As he should be universal and impartial in his rewards and approval of merits, so should he be judicial and unbending in his punishment or reproof of misconduct.'

2: YOUR OFFICERS
THE RELATIONSHIP

A Captain's relationship with his Officers has been by tradition formal. When on duty this relationship is obviously the correct one. If on the other hand you adopt a stiff attitude on all occasions, you are sacrificing one of your chief duties in your ship.

Each one of your young Officers is in his formative stage. He requires advice on almost every subject. The old system of a punctilious rebuke every month, and a punctilious commendation every 'flimsy,' does not satisfy his needs. He has often nowhere else to look for advice and inspiration except to you. You cannot give the best advice to a man standing to attention in your cabin, but you can often give it in the wardroom in general conversation, or when dispensing hospitality in your cabin, and often without his consciously knowing it.

DELEGATION OF DUTIES

As has been previously stressed, the Commanding Officer of a ship should direct and supervise. You will be judged as a Captain (with the exception of ship-handling) not on what you do yourself, but on what you inspire others to do. Your ultimate aim should not be indispensability, but the very opposite—to know that your Officers will automatically reflect your will without any verbal direction from you. Such a state of affairs, however, can obviously not be attained in a short time. Everything you delegate must naturally be supervised by you, until you reach the great day when supervision is unnecessary. Until then you should not be content until every Officer can achieve whatever task is set him as well as you could in similar circumstances yourself. Thus an untidy official letter, a large cocked hat, a ship out of station, these things must obviously not be tolerated. It must be made quite clear that when you delegate, you delegate perfection.

When an Officer realises that you have got to the stage where you can trust him without having to 'check his fixes,' then he has got half-way to command himself.

CO-ORDINATION

There is often friction in small ships between the different departments. Parochialism is a very human failing. It is your job to smooth out any difficulties between departments. Try and give the Engineroom as much consideration as the Upper Deck; when praise is due, do not only heap it on the Upper Deck. When orders are suddenly changed, do not forget to let the other departments know at the same time as the First Lieutenant.

OFFICERS' OFFENCES

As a First Lieutenant or Specialist you may have had to deal with the misdeeds of ratings; now it may be your lot to have a ship's Officer fail in his duty or comportment.

A study of court martial returns, and a catalogue of loggings over one year, would show that the great majority of offences committed by Officers are caused directly or indirectly by drink, by which is not meant drunkenness, but a lapse of duty or conduct through drink. Many of those, which appear ordinary offences in neglect of duty, are brought about by the weakening of willpower and sense of duty by drinking too much.

For this reason it is best to dwell first on this subject. As mentioned before, it is your personal example as Commanding Officer that 'calls the tune.' That you yourself may be able to drink without apparent effect is unfortunately not enough, for in all things your Officers will try to copy you. Officers have been ruined for life by getting into a habit of drinking when young, often due to the bad example set by their senior Officers.

Assuming, however, that your own particular example is good, you may still find yourself in a position where one or two of your Wardroom Officers continue to drink too much. For this reason you must be quite clear about the law.

The degree of drinking in naval messes is governed by two definite regulations in K.R. and A.I. and by two customs. The regulations are contained in Article 619(5 and 6), which restrict the wine bills of junior and warrant Officers, and in Article 1138(3), which directs the Commanding Officer to 'limit or stop any wine bills, which he may consider excessive or extravagant, having regard to the description of liquor consumed and the amount of hospitality exercised.'

There are no regulations restricting the wine bills of Officers of wardroom rank because they are considered to be sufficiently responsible to keep within reasonable limits. At the same time, it has long been the custom of the Service for Officers not to exceed a wine bill of £5 per month or to exceed a daily consumption of more than three tots of spirits. A second and excellent custom, which is rapidly becoming general throughout the Navy, is that no Officer should stand another Officer a drink, but that each Officer should pay for the liquor he consumes. This prevents Officers from standing unwanted rounds of drinks for fear of being thought ungenerous.

Your best way to enforce these regulations and to uphold these customs is to reproduce the pith of Article 619 (5 and 6) in your Standing Orders for the benefit of junior and warrant Officers, and to convey verbally or otherwise to all Officers your wish that both customs should be adhered to. In keeping with the paragraph on the framework of discipline in Chapter One, such a wish will naturally be executed.

The other offences which your Officers are likely to commit are almost invariably due to their inexperience or youthful carelessness, and in wartime, often due to a lack of mental stamina. In such cases an exact and concise representation of their errors to them in private, showing the causes and the derogatory effect on the ship, is enough to prevent repetition in all but the most thick-skinned.

THE TRAINING AND INSPIRATION OF OFFICERS

Every executive Officer in a ship is continually undergoing initiation—preparation for command himself. Therefore the inspiration of young Officers to the high standard of loyalty, leadership and consideration, which you already possess, and the increase of his general naval knowledge is one of your most important duties—in peace time your most important duty.

To take the attribute of loyalty first; so many young Officers misconstrue the full meaning of this word that you should understand its true significance. Loyalty is 'two-way.' Loyalty to the Captain is not enough. It should be bestowed in equal portions on seniors and juniors. Similarly, a Commanding Officer who is disloyal to his men—who 'passes the baby' instead of 'taking the weight'—should in justice expect an equal lack of loyalty from his junior Officers. The fact that he generally gets back a good deal more than he deserves is due to the inherent loyalty of every Naval Officer and should not blind him to the real meaning of loyalty.

With regards to loyalty to senior Officers, it will well pay you early in your command to impress on the Wardroom Officers the danger of indiscreet and idle chatter in the wardroom concerning their seniors. 'I dread not the men,' wrote Admiral Lord St. Vincent in a letter to Nelson. 'It is the indiscreet, licentious conversation of the officers, which produces all our ills.'

Leadership requires no introduction, because your Officers will acquire it by following your personal example, and because you will, it is hoped, give them every chance to acquire it.

Consideration, however, is a quality which it is often most necessary to stress. Officers must be continuously reminded of their duty toward their men. Most of the evils of modern times have arisen through the upper classes expecting privilege without obligation. Such an outlook should not exist in the Navy.

Consideration must become a habit—a way of living. There are some young Officers who are so seriously concerned with their dignity that they mistake good manners for weakness and consideration for humility. There are other Officers who—nurtured in the technical schools—imagine that 'fittings' must absorb their entire attention. Both types must be carefully guided back to the right track. Once again it is, of course, your own example which will set the high standard of consideration to the ship's company. To take one instance, as Captain you are fully entitled to order a boat at any time of the day or night, but as Captain you will not keep it waiting.

Consideration should play a tremendous part in the minds of your Officers. The ever improving standard of national education demands a higher and not a lower standard of Officer. Two hundred and fifty years ago a Captain could starve his men, insult his chaplain in public, desert his ship for months on end, and still rise to be an Admiral and a peer, as Arthur Herbert did. Nowadays we have a different outlook. We ought to be content to devote most of our thoughts to our ship's company and to serve as a Lieutenant-Commander and a commoner.

But these facts are not immediately patent to some young Officers, and it is the Captain's duty to impress them most earnestly on all.

NOTES ON EXECUTIVE TRAINING

The best training is unconscious. There are often moments on the bridge at sea when an Officer of the Watch is not fully employed. On these occasions you can carry out or delegate a programme of personal training without that Officer consciously knowing that he is learning. Often an innocently sprung question concerning, say, the deviation or some flag signal will give him considerable instruction. Commanding Officers sometimes complain of the boring hours they have to spend on the bridge. Training the young Officers is a cure for their ennui.

In harbour the junior Officers can still be kept in the picture, even if a little play acting is necessary. At the defaulters' table it may be unnecessary to hear an O.O.W's evidence, but it is of value to him if you make a point of hearing it. To send for an Officer at any time and ask him his opinion of a rating or his ideas on some suggested improvement enhances his confidence and makes him feel that you depend genuinely on him to help you.

The Officers should have access to Confidential Books and advice on which ones to read. There is, furthermore, no reason why a Commanding Officer should not extend his advice beyond the C.B. chest. Every biography, every classic read helps an Officer towards an understanding of his fellow-men, and therefore towards command.

In Lord Wavell's noted lecture on Generals he said: 'When you study military history don't read outlines on strategy or the principles of war. Read biographies, memoirs or historical novels.' Luckily for us nowadays such books are extremely entertaining, and it is not necessary to be a don in order to reach such authors as Guedalla, Ludwig, Zweig, Forester, Margaret Irwin, Winston Churchill, or Arthur Bryant.

3:YOUR MEN
THE RELATIONSHIP

Paul Jones, who was pre-eminently a Small Ship Captain, wrote of that post that a Captain should be prophet, priest, and king to his men. This was no glib aphorism, but a carefully thought out comparison. What he meant was, that the Captain is more than a mere Head-Officer. As pointed out in Part One, the Captain has definite paternal and moral obligations to the ship's company. To use an English rather than a Biblical phrase, a Captain is squire, parson, and magistrate all in one.

On assuming command it is easy to forget one of these roles. There are some Captains, for instance, who, perhaps through lack of confidence, are so bent on maintaining their detached position that they dissociate their personality entirely from the crew's personality. In doing so they are committing a psychological blunder.

Men who live together in the close company of a small ship need some corporate source of inspiration, some directive symbol to look to. The abstract symbol of Ship or Service does not fulfil this instinctive need. This feeling of trust and dedication must be vested in a person, and naturally that person should be the Captain. If, however, the Captain dissociates himself entirely from the minds of his men, each man will subconsciously seek some other source of inspiration. If he's lucky it will be a good Leading Hand. If he is unlucky it will be some old three-badge cynic. In either case the ship ceases to become a community.

There are other Captains who feel that they must stoop to conquer, who live on equal terms with their wardroom, and imagine that they can lead their men with a constant display of brotherly and well-meaning familiarity; but even Paul Jones, who fought many battles in the name of democracy, was wise enough to state that naval captaincy was essentially aristocratic. Captains who stoop are disregarding the same psychological fact as those who completely dissociate themselves. A man wants to give his trust and service to a figure right above him, and not one on his own level. He prefers his Captain to hold a lofty position. If a Captain comes off his position the crew will be the first to try and put him back there.

The art of command is therefore to be the complete master, and yet the complete friend of every man on board; the temporal lord and yet the spiritual brother of every rating; to be detached and yet not dissociated. The basis of this art is to know your men and be known by your men. It may not be possible to know each man personally, but as soon as a man realises that you know his name he begins to feel a member of the team you captain. You should certainly know your Petty Officers.

As well as the individual acquaintance of your men, you must know the 'atmosphere' of the ship. You must be close enough in touch with your ship's company to know of any feeling or rumour in the ship which may be a bad influence; for it is your job to dispel such impressions.

That your men should know you is equally important. They must know you well enough to look upon you as the trustee of their welfare on board and in their homes. Men are proverbially shy about putting in request to see Officers, and particularly the Captain. You must make it clear to the men that not only their Divisional Officers, but you yourself will do all you can for their welfare. One of the instinctive desires in every man's mind is for security. If the sailors know that you are watching over their home security you will have gone a long way towards getting a happy ship.

The men will also know you personally as the dispenser of justice. Although at Defaulters you are officially judging the other fellow, it is surprising how much judgment of you is going on at the same time. For this reason you must give infinite patience to your magisterial duties. It is often harder than you think to secure fair justice, for often an innocent sailor will put his case so badly that he will appear culpable. Only your patience will clear him.

The men will also know you indirectly in the way you handle the ship and exert your influence to bring the ship to a high standard, but it is during your ship's company talks that each and every man will get to know you best. For that reason you must look upon your talks to the crew as one of the most important things you do. The first point to realise on these occasions is that you are talking to a body of men, a number of whom are quite intelligent, and that it is the intelligent ones, and not the dull ones, who are going to criticise your speech afterwards. Therefore, while talking in simple language, you must never talk down to the men. Neither imagine that you will get the best out of a crew which you never address at all.

An intelligent man wants both information and inspiration. For this reason the Silent Skipper of last-century fiction, who in some way gained the devotion of his men by never uttering a word, will not be a success to-day. At the same time, a sailor does not want to be mustered on someone else's messdeck to hear a succession of vague and long-winded discourses on nothing in particular. Neither does he enjoy false heroics or 'flannel.' Like his tot, the sailor prefers his talks neat. For this reason, when you talk, do it at a convenient time where everybody will hear. Make certain, also, that you have something quite definite to say, and work out exactly how to say it beforehand. If Winston Churchill has to rehearse all his speeches, there is no reason why you should not.

In your talks always speak of 'we' rather than 'you.' That is the best way to get rid of the 'us-forward-them-aft' complex. Bring in all you can about ships' movements without compromising security. If you have been in action explain all you can, giving praise where due. If you have been in any large operation, use it to give the men a wider outlook, and foster a feeling of trust and admiration in the Commander-in-Chief and other senior Officers.

There is, of course, no reason to restrict information to your immediate surroundings. It is of value to a sailor if he can see himself in relation to other men. For this reason he will be interested to hear of other spheres of combat and of actions fought in different ships. Similarly, he likes to hear accounts of old naval battles or customs provided they depict the sailor of that time.

As stated before, use your talks to dispel any false rumours and to straighten out any distorted impression which the ship's company may have gathered. Napoleon saw the importance of this need, for he wrote: 'If discourses are useful, it is during the campaign; to do away with unfavourable impressions, to correct false reports, to keep alive a proper spirit in the camp, and to furnish the materials and amusements for the bivouac.'

Finally, when addressing a ship's company, Be Yourself. You cannot consistently go on being someone else for the whole commission. The sailors want to be commanded by a character, not a character sketch.

RELIGION

A Commanding Officer has religious responsibilities which are clearly laid down in K.R. and A.I.

Article 494 reads: 'The Captain is to take care that Divine Service is performed every Sunday according to the liturgy of the Church of England. . . . The Captain and all Officers and men not on duty are expected to attend this service.' Commanding Officers are also instructed to see that ratings of other denominations get every chance to attend their separate services.

In general, services outside the ship are not popular, unless the preacher is particularly good. A service on board, if intelligently conducted, has an undoubtedly good effect, for it enhances the communal spirit of the ship. But just like your ship's company talks, your services must be carefully thought out. They must mean something to the ship's company, quite a few of whom will not know the meaning of religion. If it can be arranged, try and get a chaplain on board to take your services. But in any case, if you select good hymns, apposite prayers from the Naval Prayer Book (BR. 431) and a lesson with some understandable moral or meaning, you will soon be running most popular services, and quite often the outside denominations will be joining you on the messdeck rather than going ashore.

The religious aspect of life in the Service is well described in BR. 400.

THE TRAINING AND INSPIRATION OF RATINGS

A Captain may well feel that the training of the crew for their manifold duties of vigilance and action is the responsibility of his officers. This is so, but you as Captain are the man to weld the crew into a co-ordinated fighting whole. Successful action is the result of superior team work faultlessly controlled. The majority of decorations won by Commanding Officers are won not in the half-hour of faultless control, but in the six months of training before that half-hour.

A celebrated British General, on criticising the smartness of a Guards regiment, was met with a number of excuses and complaints from the Colonel about his men, to which the General replied: 'There are no bad regiments in the brigade of Guards, Sir. Only bad Colonels.' This disconcerting remark can equally well apply to H.M. Ships. A Captain may handle a ship beautifully, read signals better than his yeoman and design a new gunsight, but these go for little unless he has the human creativeness to weld his men into a fighting unit.

A fighting ship should be composed of a number of fighting teams welded together into one big club. You are Captain of each team and president of the club.

The art of captaincy of these many teams is to give every man the subconscious incentive to do his job to his utmost. This can only be brought about by personal supervision of each team and personal understanding and encouragement to each member. It is amazing how much good you can do by a personal commendation at Sunday Divisions to an Asdic or Radar rating who made an especially good contact the week before. Once these teams feel that they are enjoying your personal interest they improve a hundredfold.

THE PETTY OFFICERS

A Commanding Officer's relationship with the Petty Officers is one of such importance that it deserves a special article. As a new Captain taking over it is an excellent introduction to the Petty Officers to gather them on their messdeck and personally read out their 'Magna Charter' (K.R. and A.I., Article 514, paragraph 6, etc.).

After this a constant impression must be fostered amongst the Petty Officers. They must realise the responsibility they carry. They are the connecting link between the Officers and the men. At present the tendency is for them to be too close to the men and too distant from the Officers. It is your duty as Captain to rectify this tendency. Accord the Petty Officers every privilege possible. Look upon misconduct in a Petty Officer as you would misconduct in an Officer. Uphold the word of a Petty Officer whenever possible. If a Petty Officer brings up a case before the O.O.D., who too lightly dismisses it, his action is bound to lower the prestige of that Petty Officer. This point must be most seriously impressed on your Officers, who should pass such cases on to the First Lieutenant.

The Coxswain should in particular hold an especial position in the ship's company. There is no reason why he should not be a Second Officer of the Watch at sea. He should be a constant link between the Captain and the messdeck. He should know of any bad feeling in any mess; of any Leading Hand who is running his mess badly. If he can have an office of his own, his position is greatly enhanced. He must have the respect, but also the confidence of the ratings. He must be capable of reprimanding any of the other Petty Officers. He must have the welfare of the ship's company consistently at heart. If the junior ratings call him 'Sir,' so much the better, and he should see that the other Petty Officers when on duty are addressed in a manner befitting their rate.

Chief Petty Officers, whenever possible, should enjoy privileges over and above those of Petty Officers.

LEADING HANDS

Due to their messing with the men the Leading Hands of a ship have a difficult job to maintain the extra dignity of their rate. Render them all the help you can with advice and privileges in giving real meaning to that word 'Leading.'

RATINGS' OFFENCES

A new Commanding Officer is bound to have difficulty over the intricate system of discipline in the Service. It is only possible here to cover the broader issue of justice. It has already been pointed out how essential it is for you to give fair judgment in every case. Below are a few points of advice which may help you.

Firstly, make a point of knowing the broad details of cases before they come up to you. This gives you a chance to study the legal aspect in advance; but, of course, it must not be allowed to tempt you to draw conclusions before seeing the case.

Secondly, you must accept a man's word unless you have circumstantial evidence that he is lying, or he definitely contradicts himself, or his word is refuted by a senior rating or Officer, or two or more ratings.

Thirdly, make a point of instructing your Junior Officers most carefully in the initial handling of serious cases. If they are in any doubt when confronted with such a case, it should be made quite clear to them that they are entitled to stand the case over until they have received advice on the matter from a more experienced Officer. Once a case has been mishandled at the outset it is often impossible to bring it back on the rails again, which means either that an offender escapes punishment or comes up for a more serious offence than that which he actually committed. The 'Officer's Aide Memoire' published for R.N.V.R. Officers should be of great help to all Junior Officers.

Fourthly, it is essential to go into the effect of a punishment on a man's career before awarding that punishment.

Fifthly, when in doubt over a case consult your Flotilla or Unit S.O., or his Secretary.

RECREATION

The recreation of a ship requires as much thought as the administration. By this we do not mean recreation in the narrow sense. Nietzsche wrote, 'Women are the recreation of warriors.' The average Naval Officer thinks more in terms of landing the Rugger Team. Neither is exactly comprehensive. Recreation should cover the whole aspect of a man's leisure hours. It should be as much intellectual recreation as physical.

Although it is generally the First Lieutenant who organises recreation, he can benefit considerably by your extra experience and guidance.

With regards to the fulfilment of Current Affairs programmes, it may not be easy to fit such sessions into the wartime routine of a small ship, but it is quite possible, and such items as local Brains Trusts and Discussion Groups have proved extremely valuable provided they are conducted by an Officer capable of keeping the discussion relevant. Another class which should enjoy your encouragement are the 'Arts and Craftsmen.' Prizes for the best ship model, the best rug, etc., do not make very large holes in your exchequer, and keep dozens of ratings creatively happy for many hours.

Recreation ashore covers the whole aspect of leave as well as games. Leave in itself deserves a few words from experience. Firstly, give all you legally can. Secondly, if prevented from granting leave see that the ship's company knows why. Thirdly, grant all-night leave, if you can, for leave until midnight is often leave broken. Fourthly, never promise leave, or even the hope of leave, until you are 100 per cent certain that it can be granted. Fifthly, do all you can to make leave ashore enjoyable by arranging trips, expeditions, dances, or games whenever possible. Sixthly, make getting ashore and returning aboard as simple and punctual as possible.

Some ships are apt to be nonplussed by local conditions; but even a desert island is not without its possibilities for recreation. The Field Games of schooldays, which entail the holding and the attempted capture of bases; sailing and fishing expeditions; swimming galas; all these keep a ship's company active and thinking instead of stagnating in a thick messdeck atmosphere.

The actual organisation of games such as football and cricket need less dissertation, as they continue automatically with no great stretch of imagination to guide them. The only advice to proffer here, is not to join eagerly in some game at which you are hopeless, under the impression that you are being a good example. The odds are that you will cause more merriment than inspiration. By all means encourage from the touch-line, but, if you play yourself, stick to the games at which you play with at least average skill.

At all times, but particularly in wartime, a small ship sailor's life, compared with a civilian life, is one of hardship. Such hardship becomes much more bearable if he knows that his superior Officers are doing all they can to get him his mails punctually, his food well cooked, his leave and shore recreation as often as possible and his leisure on board as enjoyable as possible with radio programmes, cinema programmes, tombola, 'Current Affairs' and reading material.

CONCLUSION

In conclusion, it is of interest to see how some great men of history viewed command.

Socrates

The Commander must know how to get his men their rations and every other kind of stores needed for war. He must have imagination to originate plans, practical sense and energy to carry them through. He must be observant, untiring, shrewd; kindly and cruel; simple and crafty; a watchman and a robber; lavish and miserly; generous and stingy; rash and conservative. All these and many other qualities natural and acquired, he must have. He should also, as a matter of course, know his tactics, for a disorderly mob is no more of a fighting force than a heap of building materials is a house.

Napoleon

If I always appear prepared it is because before entering on any undertaking I have meditated long and have foreseen what may occur. It is not genius which reveals to me what I should do: it is thought and meditation.

Voltaire (on Marlborough)

'That calm courage in the midst of tumult, that serenity of soul in danger, which is the greatest gift of nature for command.'

Wavell (on the qualities of a Commander)

He should have a genuine interest in, and a real knowledge of humanity; the raw material of his trade.

Loringhoven

The Officer must possess a thorough appreciation of technical science, but this must not mislead him into neglecting the study of men. Knowledge of men is a fundamental condition of successful leadership. Hence the study of History—above all of Military History—is of the highest value. It is an inexhaustible source of consolation in the midst of the monotony which is an inevitable circumstance of service in peace time.

Colonel Henderson (on Stonewall Jackson)

His supervision was constant but his interference was rare.

Education Militaire

Everything is preferable to injustice. It is better to let a guilty man escape than to risk punishing an innocent one.

Sun Tsu (B.C. 500)

Regard your men as your children, and they will follow you into the deepest valleys; look upon them as your own beloved sons and they will stand by you even unto death. If, however, you are indulgent, but unable to make your authority felt; kindhearted, but unable to enforce your commands; and incapable, moreover, of quelling disorders, then your men must be likened to spoilt children: they are useless for any practical purpose.

John Buchan (on leadership)

First there will be fortitude, the power of enduring when hope is gone, the power of taking upon oneself a desperate responsibility and daring all. There must be self-forgetfulness, a willingness to let worldly interests and even reputation and honour perish if only the task be accomplished. The man who is concerned with his own repute will never move mountains. There must be patience, supreme patience under misunderstandings and setbacks and the muddles and interferences of others. There must be resilience in defeat, a manly optimism which looks at all the facts in all their bleakness and yet dares to hope. There must be a sense of the eternal continuity of a great cause, so that failure will not seem the end, and a man sees himself as only a part in a predestined purpose. . . . Leadership, then, depends primarily upon moral endowments.

Collingwood (on liquor)

Every day affords you instances of the evils arising from drunkenness. Were a man as wise as Solomon and as brave as Achilles, he would still be unworthy of trust if he addicted himself to grog. He may make a drudge, but a respectable Officer he can never be; for the doubt must always remain that the capacity which God has given him will be abused by intemperance.

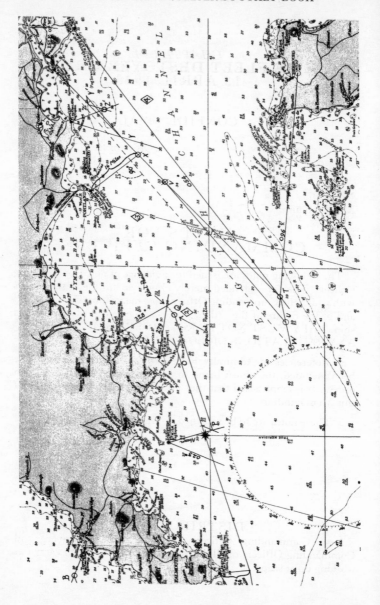

CHAPTER VI
HOME FLEET DESTOYER ORDERS
15 APRIL 1943

CONFIDENTIAL

Office of Rear Admiral (D),
Home Fleet,
C/o G.P.O.

No.H.D.3.
Memorandum.

London
15th April, 1943.

NOTES FOR
COMMANDING OFFICERS

The following notes are issued for guidance of new Commanding Officers. They are intended merely to give an outline of the orders with which the Commanding Officer must make himself acquainted, and of the nature of the orders which he himself must issue in his ship. THEY MUST NOT BE REGARDED AS OVER-RIDING ANY REGULATIONS OR LOCAL ORDERS.

2. References to Admiralty Fleet Orders and other orders have been included, the object being to point out the existence of such orders. It is emphasised that they are only up to date at the date of this Memorandum.

3. These notes are to be returned on leaving Scapa.

I.G. GLENNIE.
Rear Admiral (D),
Home Fleet.

DISTRIBUTION.

New Commanding Officers of home fleet destroyers and Commanding Officers of all destroyers and sloops due to carry out working up at scapa.

1: SAFETY OF THE SHIP

Both in peace and in war the first responsibility of a Captain is the safety of his ship.

Risking collision or grounding is no more justified in war than in peace, unless by so doing you can further the destruction of the enemy.

2. **Anchor Watch.** When at anchor never hesitate to raise steam and set watch if you have any doubt about the weather. The ship is yours to look after, so do not wait for orders.

3. **Chart Work.** Many a good ship has been lost owing to:—

(a) Uncorrected charts. Q.Zs should be placed on charts as soon as received. See also H.D.325.

(b) Placing unwarranted trust in small scale charts.

(c) Errors in transferring the ship's position from one chart to another.

(d) Using the wrong scale of distance—particularly after transferring to a new chart.

4. **Lights.** Commanding Officer should be conversant with H.D.335.

5. **Mines.** Commanding Officer should be conversant with the information given in C.B.03056 and on Charts Z.27A and B also Secret Chart Z.36. Z.27A and B should be on the bridge at sea in Pilotage Waters.

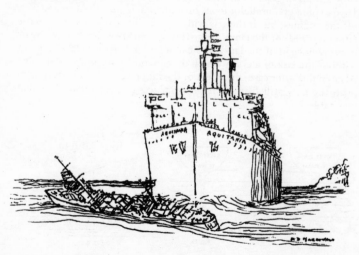

2: NOTES ON SHIP HANDLING

The prestige of a Captain of a small ship is much enhanced if he handles his ship well. Chapter VII of 'Remarks on Handling Ships'—O.U.5274—is worth reading.

2. **Safety First.** The necessity for avoiding minor damage to your ship is naturally of importance always, but it is of paramount importance in war time, when not only are the repair services strained to the utmost, but we cannot afford to have ships in unspectacular fashion than to risk a crash by performing a spectacular manoeuvre.

3. **The Alternative.** Whenever and wherever you are going to secure your ship—to a buoy, oiler, jetty, etc.—always make up your mind exactly what you are going to do. Moreover, in addition always have an alternative in case your projected manoeuvre does not go according to plan owing to wind, tide, or sea. The majority of crashes occur owing to not having taken this elementary precaution. It is generally too late to start thinking about the alternative once things have gone wrong.

4. **Approach Angle.** Coming alongside an oiler or other ship, the approach should be made at a fairly broad angle (about 30°), with your ship's head pointing at her stem or even further ahead. If you do this, you make certain of getting your head rope across the first time and having secured, then work your stern in with the engines. If you come up parallel it looks nice to go half speed astern and ring off the engines; but if there is wind or tide it is extremely easy to be either too wide or too close. If the former you are unlikely to get your heaving lines in, if the latter you cannot alter out at the last moment without the risk of a crash which may involve your inner propellor. Also, in the latter case, the effect of the inner screw going astern is to push the bow still further in thus making a crash forward almost inevitable.

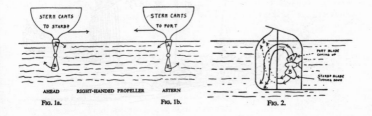

FIG. 1a.   FIG. 1b.   FIG. 2.

5. **Oiler Yawing.** Coming alongside an oiler when it is blowing, and she is yawing, the best time to make your approach is when your ship will be steaming exactly head to wind, as obviously she will then steer better at slower speed. The moment is worth waiting for.

6. **Straight Run.** Always give yourself as much room as possible for your approach, so that you can have a straight run up to your buoy or alongside if possible. It is often very tempting to try and save time by cutting the corner, but if this means that your approach will be made with the ship still swinging the chances are that you will lose time and not gain it.

7. **Heaving Lines.** Heaving lines should be thrown *only once* to reach their mark. All sailors think they can throw a heaving line about twice as far as they really can, and must be well drilled to make certain of it first time. In bad weather do not forget the Coston Gun—it's what it's there for, but some people seem to think they 'lose face' by using it.

8. **Scapa Rough Weather Anchorages.** At Scapa, if after being out for exercises or at sea, the weather has got worse and you are doubtful about picking up your buoy, do not wait to ask permission to anchor in shelter, and certainly do not think that you *must* 'have one shot at it, anyway'. It is up to you to decide what you intend, act on it, and say you are doing it. Far better to anchor and have done with it, than have your whaler down and irretrievable and eventually go ashore on Flotta or Fara.

Foul weather anchorages are:—

(i)   In Northerly gales—Under North shore in vicinity of Orphir Bay.

(ii) In Southerly gales—Close North of Hunda.

Note:—Berths referred to in (ii) are laid down in H.W.O.50, paragraph 8.

9. **Gutter Sound.** The traffic problem in Gutter Sound becomes progressively more difficult as the traffic increases with increased war production and the development of the Base. Make your signalmen keep a vigilant look out for traffic and signals, not forgetting the floating dock. The references in local orders are:—

Scapa General Order 11—Navigation in Gutter Sound.

                        12—Destroyer Speeds past Floating Dock.

D.T.M. 236—Limitation of speed at Scapa.

Other references in local orders are:—

Scapa Temporary Memorandum 200—Gutter Sound Roundabout.

D.T.M.   279—Seamanlike precautions in Harbour.

10. **Orders for working main engines.** There are no hard and fast rules on this subject, but the following orders are suggested as a basis as they have worked well in practice:—

(i) Engine Telegraph Speed Indication.

SLOW means . . . . . . Revolutions for about 5 knots.

HALF means . . . . . . Revolutions as indicated by revolution telegraph.

FULL means . . . . . . As fast as possible accepting possible damage to machinery.

These meanings apply equally to orders AHEAD and ASTERN.

Notes:—

(a) 'Full Speed' will only be used in an emergency when the immediate safety of the ship is in danger. If a rapid increase of power is required under any other conditions, the telegraph should be kept at 'HALF' and the revelations greatly increased.

(b) The astern power that can be developed will only be about one third that of the ahead power.

(ii) Safeguarding Telegraph after Trial. Moving Wheel. Finishing with Engines.

Special Sea Dutymen should be piped to their stations some time before commencing the weigh or slipping. The Quartermaster and Telegraphsmen will thus be present when the Engineer Officer tries the Telegraphs and steering gear. The Quartermaster and Telegraphsmen are responsible that the telegraphs are not moved again after the trial is completed.

The Officer of the Watch is responsible that the order 'Obey the Telegraphs' is passed at least two minutes before the engines will be required. He is, however, to ask the Captain's permission before passing this order.

When the Engine Room has received the order 'Obey the Telegraphs', they are to report 'Standing By'. Normally no engine movements will be ordered by the forebridge until this report has been received.

In the event of the Engine Room observing the telegraphs being moved before the order 'Obey the Telegraphs' has been passed they are at once to ring up the Forebridge and request instructions.

The Quartermaster on watch is responsible that the wheel is moved one or two degrees every ten minutes from the time he closes up, in order to circulate the oil which is being churned by the steering motor.

It is of great importance that the engine room telegraphs and revolution indicator should be tested regularly as a routine, when the ship is about to go to sea and also daily at sea.

11. Oiling by buoyant hose.

All ships will be required to exercise oiling by buoyant hose from oilers. This will be arranged during the work-up period. Commanding Officers should study B.R.853. Pages 4 and 9 of the B.R. state that the steadying line should be kept slack; this may not always be possible, but the guiding principle should be to regard the steadying line as a marker, rather than as a towing point.'

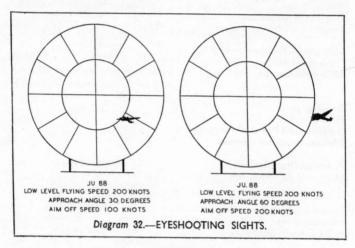

JU 88
LOW LEVEL FLYING SPEED 200 KNOTS
APPROACH ANGLE 30 DEGREES
AIM OFF SPEED 100 KNOTS

JU.88
LOW LEVEL FLYING SPEED 200 KNOTS
APPROACH ANGLE 60 DEGREES
AIM OFF SPEED 200 KNOTS

Diagram 32.—EYESHOOTING SIGHTS.

3: HEADINGS FOR SHIP'S ORDERS

The following list gives the more important points which must be considered in organising your ship for service. It will certainly not be necessary to write orders on every subject but they must be thought over if you are to act quickly when emergencies arise.

1. General Orders.	Reference.
Secrecy Regulations.	C.A.F.O.'s.
Magazine Regulations.	N.M. & E.R.
Magazine flooding and spraying.	N.M. & E.R. and Handbook of Ammunition (O.U. 5463).
Fire Service, pumping and flooding.	
Steering failures.	
Collision and Grounding, and Captain's Reports.	K.R. and A.I.
Fog—Signalling and Navigation.	

Use of D.G. coils and compass
  correctors.   C.A.F.O's and D.T.O. 142.
Accoustic Mines—precautions.   H.W.O.38, C.A.F.O.2172/42.
Marking and closing of W/T doors.   Damage Control Handbook.
Darkening Ship.   Local organisation.
Ventilation and prevention of sweating.
Anti-gas and decontamination.   O.U.5427(38).
Safety of Ship's company at sea.   Local organisation. D.T.M.149.
Taking in tow.
Buoying of wrecks, etc.   U-boats. . . . C.A.F.O.381/41.
Demolition ashore and at sea.   B.R.153 and 153(2), D.T.O's 137
                                               and 137a.

Unexploded Bombs—general
  information.
Midget submarines.   Monthly anti-submarine reports
                                               and ciphers. (For U-boats see
                                               paragraph 2 below.)

Boarding parties.
Prize Crews.
Survivors and Prisoners—segregation.
Precautions against sabotage.

2. Action Organisation.   **Reference.**
Degrees of Readiness.   Handbook of Gunnery
                                               Organisation; D.T.O.51., D.F.I.
                                               Section XVIII.

Lookouts (also lighting of
compartments).
Recognition of Aircraft.   Silhouette books, posters, 'A'
                                               messages.

Control of Fire for
  (a) L.A. Targets   Destroyer Firing Manual and H.D.
                                               452(c) dated 28.12.42. (Concentra
                                               tion see also D.T.O.52.)
  (b) A.A. Targets.)   (H.A. Firing Manual.
      Barrage Fire.)   (C.A.F.O.2361/40, D.T.O.55,
                                               H.T.O.63.
  (c) 'E' Boats.   D.T.O.3.
  (d) Divided control for dive
      bombing.   Local organisation; D.T.O.51.
Night Action—Searchlight—star shell.   Destroyer Firing Manual,
                                               D.T.O.56.
Ammunition—supply—types of shell.   Handbook of ammunition.
Spare gear.
Depth Charge stations and settings.   O.U.5485, C.B.4097 (10).
A/S.   C.B.4097.
Boarding and Salvage of U-boats.   C.A.F.O.2469/41 (amended by
                                               C.A.F.O.35'42.)

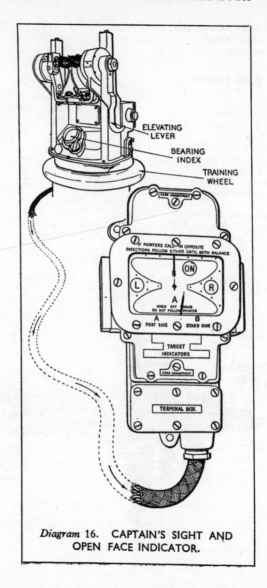

Diagram 16. CAPTAIN'S SIGHT AND
OPEN FACE INDICATOR.

Smoke floats—C.S.A. gear.
Torpedoes (if fitted).   D.T.O., Section III.
Flank marking.   D.T.O.54.

3. Battle Orders.   Reference.
Dealing with fire.   )   C.A.F.O.720/41
Fire and Repair parties.)   (H.D. 00301 of 10/3/40.)
Damage Control.   )   Damage Control Handbook and
Shoring bulkheads.   )   A.F.O. P.288/40.
Electrical supply.
Emergency supply.
Secondary lighting.
Food in action.
Sanitary arrangements.   Local organisation.
Treatment of wounded.   M.D.G's Memo 'Treatment of
                                 Casualties'.

Ramming and Boarding.
Disposal of C.B.'s and S.P.'s   C.B. Form U2D(41), Article 33.
Destruction of Asdic Set.   C.A.F.O. 161/42.
Abandon Ship.
Sinking Ship.   D.T.O.42.

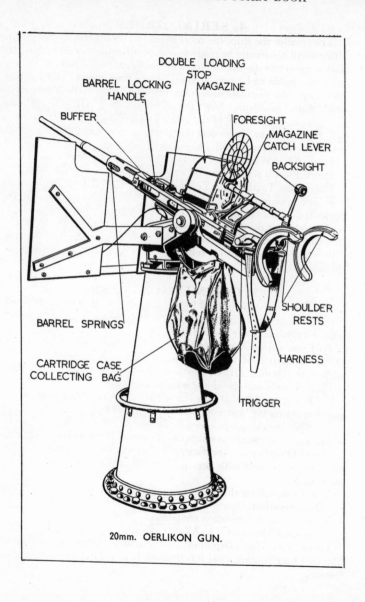

20mm. OERLIKON GUN.

4: SERIAL ORDERS

The smaller the ship, the more serial orders she has to cope with. Efforts will constantly be made to reduce their number and contents, and suggestions to this effect will be welcomed. Destroyers are, however, liable to be sent at short notice on a variety of jobs, and must carry the requisite orders, as they carry the charts to get there.

2. Two problems face the Commanding Officer in this connection—knowledge of the various orders and their correction.

3. **Knowledge.** The orders relating to tactical handling of his ship must be known fairly well, i.e.:—

Home Fleet War Orders. (H.W.O.)
Home Fleet Tactical Instructions. (F.T.I.)
Destroyers Tactical and Technical Orders. (D.T.O.)

4. The remainder should be regarded as books of reference to be consulted when required. Commanding Officers need only know their way about these orders, and what they contain.

5. **Correction.** A Writer should be trained to correct all non-secret orders and O.U's and thus relieve officers of all but supervision of this work.

5: COMMUNICATIONS

You are sure to be judged by the signals you originate. Take an interest in other authorities' signals—notice their priorities and addresses; when to use code or cypher.

2. If you depart from your instruction at sea, keep your Senior Officer informed of your movements. Consider if breaking W/T silence is justified. If W/T silence is broken always give your position, course and speed and a weather report.

3. Do not 'propose' if you really mean 'intend'. Avoid as far as possible asking for 'instructions'.

4. The working-up period is for the benefit of your communication ratings as much as for the rest of the ship's company.

The H.O's will not be proficient at reading morse to start with, but must be impressed with the need for alertness and quickness in answering.

A smart signalling ship soon earns a wide reputation.

5 **Organisation.**

See that your organisation covers:—

(a) General Messages. (A, AZ, QZ, Z, etc.)

These are *Most Important*. A missing Admiralty General Message may contain vital information (e.g. change of recognition system).

It is advisable to have a list of originator's numbers displayed in the S.D.O. so that missing numbers and those last received can be seen at a glance. Ensure that you always keep 'close up' in harbour; it is not safe to rely on the automatic receipt of these messages from shore authorities.

(b) Recognition Signals.

Responsibility for making out and checking the current signals, setting the VC/VF, etc.

(c) S.P's and C.B.'s.

(i) Officer responsible for muster (G.S.I., Part I X 5).

(ii) The issue at the right time of new publications coming into force.

(iii) The destruction of these books in deep and shallow waters. (G.S.I., Part I X 6).

Note:—You should take a personal interest in this dull but important subject. Mistakes may lead to serious consequences. (See also Section VI.)

6. Enemy Reporting.

All Officers of the Watch, Telegraphists and Signalmen should be capable of making out as Enemy Report correctly, i.e. Self Evident Code Reports, Help Messages, and Reports of Aircraft, including Shadowers.

7. Recognition.

All Officers of the Watch and Signalmen must also be conversant with ALL forms of Recognition Procedure (S.P.02220(2) and latest A Messages).

These include Identification Marks, Recognition Procedure with Merchant Vessels and with Minor War Vessels; Entry into Defended Ports, both those with Port War and War Signal Stations (C.A.F.O.478/41).

8 Ship's Position.

Internal organisation must allow for the W/T Office to have the ship's position, course and speed:—

(a) At the beginning of each watch, in Latitude and Longitude for Distress Messages (in Fleet Code).

(b) Each hour in Lettered Co-ordinates, for Self Evident Enemy Reports.

9. W/T Messages.

At sea, it is useful to know as soon as a signal addressed to you is in the ship.

Also, it is useful to know when a message that you have originated is cleared to a shore station.

10. 'After Action'.

Check up on W/T *and* V/S 'after action' arrangements, and the facilities available if all ship's power is lost.

If practicable, keep an Aldis Lamp and battery aft.

11. Before going to sea, be sure of:—

(a) Recognition Signals in force (S.P.02220(2) and latest A Messages.

(b) W/T Organisation: Area and Port waves required.

(c) How Enemy surface craft, submarines or aircraft should be reported, and think out specimen reports. (F.S.B., Section 4, and A.F.O. S.2.)

12. Before proceeding to sea with Fleet Units be sure of:—

(a) Screening Diagrams and Instructions for Screens. C.O.F., Chapter XI, as amended by S.P.C.31/43.

(b) Methods of altering course—Red PT, Signals BW and EP—when to change sides (C.O.F., Chapter VIII and Article 357).

(c) Alarm Signals and associated pyrotechnic and sound signals. (F.S.B., Section 4.)

(d) Zig-Zags. (B.R.248 and C.O.F., Articles 143 and 144.)

(e) Conduct of the Fleet in Fog. (C.O.F., Chapter IV, Article 16, et seq.)

(f) W/T Organisation, and the use of Short Range W/T. (A.F.O. S.2 or H.W.C.O's.)

(g) Enemy Reporting, when in company. (H.W.C.O's.)

13. Before proceeding to sea with a Convoy, look up:—

(a) Escort Diagrams (A.C.I's).

(b) Alter Course Signals, including Emergency Turns. (Mersigs.)

(c) Alarm and pyrotechnic signals. (Mersigs.)

(d) Zig-Zags. (B.R.248 and Mersigs (N.B. Procedure differs from that in C.O.F.)).

(e) Conduct in Fog. (Mersigs.)

(f) W/T and R/T organisation, including communications with aircraft. (W.A.S.O.)

(g) D/F watch for U-boats (latest A messages).

14. On arrival in harbour, find out:—

(a) W/T watch required. (H.W.C.O's or local orders.)

(b) Restrictions on use of W/T, and use in fog or emergency. (H.W.C.O's or local orders.)

(c) V/S watch required. (H.W.C.O's or local orders.)

(d) How Air Raid Warning Signals are received and whether additional W/T watch will be required on their receipt. (H.W.C.O's or local orders.)

(e) Consider whether signalmen of watch should have authority to press alarm rattlers.

15. Coding and cyphering.

Full instructions concerning all coding and cyphering matters are contained in A.F.O. S.66/43.

16. D/F.

For a good bearing always turn BOWS on. Bearings at night may not be as good as those obtained by day. For all details of D/F stations, procedure for obtaining bearings, etc., see D/F instructions in A.F.O. S.2 Enemy D/F of homing submarines.

17. R.D.F.

Good results cannot be expected until operators develop 'sea sense' and have an idea of what is happening outside. When not required for operating, they are best employed as lookouts in order to learn the appearance of A/S screens, the effect of zig-zagging, etc.

Officers of the Watch should give every assistance to R.D.F. operators and assist them in identifying various types of target; liaison between the director and Type 285 must also be encouraged if effective results are to be obtained.

18. Personnel.

(a) **Signalmen and Telegraphists.**

Advancement   —A.F.O's 885/43, 886/43, 6376/42 and 432/42.
Higher Grade Courses   —A.F.O's 6256/42 (for 1943 courses)
Examinations   —Home fleet General Orders.

(b) **Coders.**

Advancement   —A.F.O's 5257/42, 885/43 and former A.F.O's.

(c) **R.D.F. ratings.**

Advancement   —A.F.O's 4496/42, 6115/42 and 6258/42.

(d) **Radio Mechanics.**

C.A.F.O. 66/42.

6: CORRESPONDENCE

Rules. See D.T.M. 66 and D.O.91, and C.A.F.O. 306/42. General rules are laid down in K.R. and A.I., Articles 874-886. Note in particular number of copies required; failure to comply leads to a lot of extra and unnecessary work.

2. **Returns.** These are listed in D.L.R. 'Hasteners' should not be looked upon as rebukes, but as helpful reminders.

3. **Return of Orders on leaving Scapa.** (See D.T.M.136.)
Orders should be returned direct to issuing authorities.

W.A.S.O's Part III should be retained on board unless the ship is proceeding to operate from an east coast port when they should be returned to Commander-in-Chief, Western Approaches.

4. **Confidential Books and Documents.** Instructions are contained in C.B. Form U2.D. Confidential books are to be under the charge of a **Commissioned Officer**, who should make himself fully conversant with the instructions for their custody. Records of receipt, destruction, etc. should be made *at the time*, and particular care should be taken when destroying books that only those authorised to be destroyed are included.

5. The care of these books, etc. is the Commanding Officer's responsibility. This is a very unsatisfactory way of coming to grief, which can be avoided by seeing that proper attention is given to their care.

6. With reference to C.A.F.O. 1603/41, paragraph 7, inspections of ships' C.B. and S.P. organisations will be carried out by an Officer on the staff of Rear Admiral (D), Home Fleet towards the end of the working-up period.

7. **Wartime Reports.** In addition to references shown in Home Fleet List of Returns (H.L.R.) and other publications, the following is a list of some orders calling for special reports or action to be taken on certain occasions. It may be found useful for ready reference *but it cannot be considered exhaustive* and will have to be kept up to date if it is to continue to be of value.

Unless otherwise stated, references are to Admiralty Fleet Orders and Confidential A.F.O's (prefix C.):—

Air Attacks by the Enemy.	C. 595/41
Ammunition, Reports of Expenditure after action.	C. 305/40

Attacks on U-boats.	C. 3344/39
	C. 3774/39
	C. 4/40
Attacks on Escorted Convoys—Signal to be made on breaking W/T silence.	C. 380/41
Damage to Ships.	C.2972/39
	C. 3967/39
	C. 889/40
Damage to ships by mines.	C. 1968/40
Damage to Machinery.	C. 3833/39
Damage to Gun Armament Material.	C. 112/40
Damage to Electrical Installations.	C. 3376/39
Enemy W/T transmission.	C. 381/40
Engagements with the Enemy.	C. 1045/40
Loss of H.M. Ships.	3700/40
Loss of H.M. Ships—disposal of S.P's and C.B's.	C. 1178/40
Minelaying by Enemy Aircraft.	C. 1849/40
Prisoners of War.	2036/40
	2358/40
	2898/40
	3029/40
	C. 1553/40
	C. 2/41
Removal of Enemy Aliens from Neutral Ships.	C. 539/41
Shell, Functioning of, in Action.	C. 3937/39
Submarines, Treatment of by Warships.	C. 725/41
Weather—Report when breaking W/T silence.	See Section IV.

7: PUNISHMENTS

Copies of (i) H.F. Form 3 (Punishments and Punishment Returns) and (ii) Commander-in-Chief, Home Fleet's Memorandum No.H.F.167/86 of 28th February, 1941 (Punishments for Leave Breaking Offences), are enclosed. The latter is a guide only, as stated in paragraph 2 of the Memorandum.

2. **Reduction to Second Class for Conduct.** A.F.O.206/41 authorises reduction to the second class for conduct for desertion or serious leave breaking offences. Full use should be made of this, which is an alternative to losing a man's services while in detention, and possibly causing him to miss dangerous or arduous service. (See A.F.O.4492/41.)

3. **Suspension of Sentences.** Commanding Officers should consider in suitable cases whether to suspend sentence of detention. The procedure is shown in K.R. and A.I., Article 471b and 559. Sentences may be suspended when a man of previous excellent character has committed himself as the result of long-continued strain, or in circumstances which render him deserving of a chance of retrieving his character, or when a man's services are required for an arduous or dangerous duty which he would otherwise avoid. The three-monthly review (pending final remission) should not be missed—K.R. & A.I. Article 559 (11).

When a summary punishment of imprisonment or detention is suspended the offence(s) and punishment(s) should nevertheless be entered in the current punishment return, and the punishment warrant read and forwarded with the return, with a note that the punishment has been suspended. (See A.F.O. 2016/42, notification on discharge to another ship or establishment).

4. See also A.F.O.4311/40 and 1160/41 regarding consequential penalties.

5. **Investigation of serious offences.** See H.F. Form 3, paragraphs 1-5.

Note the desirability of medical evidence in all cases of (i) striking; (ii) drunkedness; (iii) unnatural offences.

6. Having been warned, and made a voluntary statement, the accused *Must Not Be Asked Any Questions*, except to clear up points in what he has already said.

7. **'Former Acquittal or Conviction'.** It is a principle of law that a man should not be put in peril more than once for the same offence.

8. When a case is likely to be tried by Court Martial, therefore, the Commanding Officer must not say or do anything at the preliminary investigation which indicates that he went beyond mere enquiry and tried the case himself. He must not, for example, forward a punishment warrant or application for dismissal, or announce his intention of doing so. An investigation should be terminated with the order 'Remanded' not 'Punished by warrant'.

9. If a Commanding Officer is in any doubt as to whether a case should be dealt with by Court Martial instead of summarily, he should consult his Senior Officer before taking any action, either verbally or by letter.

10. **Imprisonment and Detention at Scapa.** See A.F.O.4103/42, H.G.O.180 and O.S.O.B.11.

Accommodation and escort for ratings sentenced to imprisonment or detention are arranged by Rear Admiral (D), the ship being informed of the time the rating should be sent on board *Dunluce Castle* for passage south. Offenders are sent South on Tuesdays and Fridays.

When, through lack of accommodation, ratings are sentenced to imprisonment in lieu of detention, the directions given in C.A.F.O. 11/41 Remission Rules—should be observed.

The ship to which the offender belongs is responsible for preparing and forwarding a Committal Warrant with each offender sent to imprisonment or detention.

Imprisonment, as such, should not be awarded to a rating whom it is proposed to retain in the Service. A mere intention to ask for discharge S.N.L.R. is not considered justification for awarding imprisonment.

11. **Cells at Scapa.** See O.S.O.B. 12. A signal should be made to H.M.S. *Tyne* requesting accommodation. If, and only if, none is available, a further signal should be made to H.M.S. *Iron Duke*, (R) A.C.O.S.

Ships having offenders for cell punishment are always to ensure that a cell is available in either *Tyne* or *Iron Duke* before reading the warrant. If it is not available offenders are normally to be retained on board until it is, whether the ship is required to go to sea or not.

Only in very exceptional cases will permission be given for offenders to be discharged to *Tyne* to await accommodation.

See H.F. Form 3, paragraph 31, 'Certificate of Medical Fitness'.

12. **Offences against the Censorship Regulations.** Notes for guidance in the framing of charges for offences against the censorship regulations are contained in O.S.O.B. 20, paragraph 4. (See also H.G.O. 26).

13. **Ask advice when in doubt.** If in doubt as to degree or nature of punishment to be awarded, or as to any other points concerning discipline or correspondence, Rear Admiral (D)'s staff are always ready to offer advice. Write, or better still, call and see Rear Admiral (D)'s Secretary.

8: ACTION MESSING IN DESTROYERS

Napoleon's adage that a man cannot fight on an empty stomach still holds good, and in this war prolonged periods of action stations at sea are inevitable sooner or later.

2. There are two conditions of service to meet:—

(a) When there is ample warning, for example before an assault supported by the Navy.

(b) The unexpected, for example chase and destruction of the *Scharnhorst*.

3. In either circumstance it is necessary to have organisation.

(i) The Senior Supply rating should have an action station in which he is accessible.

(ii) At least one reliable cook or steward should be in the forward and after repair parties in charge of food.

(iii) An action cook should be detailed from each quarters who can best be spared.

(iv) Some space should be earmarked forward and aft for stowage of the food required. For example, the Issue room forward, the Wardroom pantry or provision room aft; but there are obviously many possibilities.

4. Action Messing with Prior Warning

The requirements of secrecy will probably preclude much preparation before the ship sails, but once this is no longer paramount an extra one or two days' issue of fresh meat or corned beef, potatoes and flour can be made to each mess and prepared to the same recipe. The galley then works overtime preparing such foods as cornish pasties, sausage rolls, sandwiches, etc., which are distributed fore and aft on a general mess system. The mess supplies of tea, sugar, etc., are pooled and distributed fore and aft according to numbers.

Issue of additional messtraps is not recommended as they are likely to be lost but Leading Hands of messes can be made responsible for a limited quantity at their action stations and if conditions are bad, breakages can be written off.

Provisions issued in this manner should be charged to messes. This can be done by pricing the whole of the issues and charging the messes in accordance with numbers borne. The total quantities issued should be entered in red on page 6, line 18 of the Provision Account and the money value entered in the Mess Book against individual messes. A certificate showing details should accompany the Provision Account.

5. Action Messing in Emergency

To allow for sudden action stations which is unforeseen and lasts for a long period it is essential in destroyers to have a supply of action food at both ends of the ship.

A supply of corned beef, tinned meat, tea, sugar, milk, cocoa and tinned fruit is suggested.

Provisions consumed in lieu of normal victualling should be charged against messes in accordance with numbers borne but (in this instance, if difficulty arises), additional quantities including tinned fruits should be written off as extra issues under K.R. 1825 on the signature of the Commanding Officer.

6. Hot Drinks

In Northern waters when weather is frequently bad, the provision of hot drinks requires careful thought. A certain amount of water can be boiled using Electric Kettles and radiators, but as galley fires must be drawn this is only a makeshift.

The question of providing a steam jet, which could be taken to the ship's Company and Officers' Galleys fore and aft, is under investigation.

7. Action Rations

Instructions for the maintenance and issue of action rations (tins of Horlicks and barley sugar tablets and chewing gum) are contained in A.F.O. 1909/43.

8. Hot Weather Messing

Special instructions regarding action messing under hot weather conditions are contained in C.A.F.O. 1991/42.

CHAPTER VII
MUTINY IN THE ROYAL NAVY
Notes on Dealing with Mutiny or
Massed Disobedience, AUGUST 1944

CONFIDENTIAL

This book is invariably to be kept locked up when not in use, and is not to be taken outside the ship or establishment to which it is issued without the express permission of the Commanding Officer.

Mutinies or massed disobedience have their origin in discontent which is the result of some real or fancied grievance or hardship. The accumulated experience of past years is set forth in C.B. 3027 ('Mutiny in the Royal Navy,' Volume I), the lessons of which may be summarized as follows:—

2. The most likely causes of discontent can be divided into two groups:—

Those caused by **Internal** events within the ship:—

(*a*) Indifferent food or broken meal hours.

(*b*) Irksome and uncertain routines.

(*c*) Unusual working hours when the necessity is not evident or has not been explained.

(*d*) Uncomfortable living and working conditions.

Events normally controlled from sources **External** to the ship:—

(*e*) Curtailment or cancellation without any evident reason of expected leave.

(*f*) Apparent discrimination between different ships, squadrons or classes of men in working or living conditions and routines.

(*g*) Irregular mails.

(*h*) Alleged inadequacy of or injustice in pay or allowances, including allowances for wives and children, and unexplained or avoidable delays in payment.

It is worthy of note that events in the second group are generally of slow growth—a pressure is gradually built up by a growing sense of injustice.

Discontent arising from causes in the first group is likely to be more spontaneous and such causes may well provide the spark which ignites a more deep-seated sense of grievance.

It is therefore clearly desirable that, if external events should cause incipient feelings of discontent, C.O.s should give careful thought to the avoidance of internal events which might flare up and cause an outbreak of insubordination out of all proportion to the degree of importance of the act which set the disobedience in motion.

3. It is the duty of Officers to endeavour to avoid the development of any grievance into discontent. They should do all in their power to remove the grievance, explain it away where it is ill-founded or represent it to higher authority where the remedy is outside their control. Particularly should explanation be given to the men of the need for any measures which may be expected to lead to complaint if the reasons for them are not understood. Action of this kind stimulates the all important factor of confidence felt by men of the lower deck in the ability of their Officers to remedy or represent their grievances, and further that such grievances, when represented, will receive the close and immediate attention of superior officers and the Board of Admiralty. It is essential that Officers develop this confidence.

4. The trouble to be considered may range from organized refusal of duty by a few men to mutiny, with or without violence, by a large part of a ship's company. Whatever form it may take, the broad outline of the appropriate method of dealing with it is the same, though it is well to be prepared for the worst case, particularly as a relatively minor incident may develop suddenly into serious trouble.

5. Should there be any evidence of general discontent which might develop into massed disobedience, or if such disobedience occurs, the action of all Officers must be such as to indicate unmistakeably that they intend to retain or regain control and to uphold discipline. Prompt action must be taken at the same time to make it clear to the men that their grievances will be investigated and, if found to be genuine, remedied with as little delay as possible, provided they carry out their duties.

6. Ringleaders should be drastically and immediately dealt with, leniency might, after a suitable pause, be shown to the remainder. A ringleader should never be pardoned or treated leniently because he is a 'good hand'; such men are all the more dangerous on that account. (*See* C.B. 3027, p. 149, Lord St. Vincent's opinion.)

7. When massed disobedience is suspected or occurs, the following broad rules are suggested as governing the action to retain or to regain control:—

(i) Agitators will almost certainly make use of propaganda, and early steps should be taken to obtain information as to what is going on, with a view to countering action of this type. Full use should be made of Petty Officers and Leading Rates to bring sound influence to bear on the lower ratings.

(ii) Disaffected men and ships or squadrons should be isolated so far as practicable from loyal men and unit.

(iii) Steps should be taken to ensure that any ships not in company, and which may be assumed to be loyal, are not allowed to join up with disaffected ships, unless their presence is considered necessary or desirable.

(iv) To frustrate attempts by disloyal elements in one ship to influence men in other ships, very thorough steps should be taken to prevent illicit communication by Visual Signalling, Wireless Telegraphy, etc. Boats should be guarded, leave restricted, canteens and other meeting places picketed, and demonstrations on the forecastle or in other prominent positions prevented. These points are of the greatest importance since they cause loss of that confidence which knowledge of support in other ships engenders.

(v) In order to indicate clearly that the officers intend to maintain or regain control, the Executive Officer, accompanied by some Officers and Petty Officers, should himself, if necessary, proceed to the seat of the demonstration and take charge of the situation.

(vi) It can be assumed that a large number of the men are not only loyal, but do not wish to have anything to do with the disloyal element. Steps should, therefore, be taken at once to divide the loyal from the disloyal and to keep them apart. The earliest opportunity should be made of taking the names of disloyal men or of identifying at least some of the more prominent ones.

(vii) When the loyal have been separated from the disloyal, every endeavour should be made to win over men who still remain disloyal. A minority can exercise considerable intimidation and there will always be men who will welcome a safe opportunity to retrieve their original lapse. Should the men respond to the presence of the Executive Officer, they may either be ordered to proceed to their duty or to fall in. If they are fallen in they must not be allowed to mass but must invariably be divided into units such as watches and parts of the ship, the Senior Rating of each small party taking charge and Petty Officers carrying out supervision under Divisional Officers.

(viii) Whether it is desirable for the Commanding Officer then to address the men concerned, or whether to address the whole ship's company, is a matter for judgment depending on the circumstances, but should he address them he should start by warning them of the seriousness of their mass action and the discredit it brings on the ship and themselves, and remind them of the authorised channel by which they can express grievances. The innate loyalty of the Petty

Officers and men should inevitably respond. The Captain, as the final authority, should not intervene at too early a stage, but having taken charge, he should remain in personal control until the situation has eased.

(ix) Before the whole company is addressed by the Captain, all Chief and Petty Officers should, unless there is reason to doubt the loyalty of any of them, be fallen in and informed of the situation and of the line of action which the Captain proposes to take. The object of this is to (a) show the lower ratings that all authority is united, and (b) impress their responsibilities on the higher ratings and give them a sense of confidence in the power of the authority they wield.

(x) When addressing the men, it is as well to do so from the opposite direction to that expected. Ringleaders will almost certainly have placed themselves in the background, whence they can interrupt with impunity, and if they find themselves in the front rank, their influence will be considerably reduced and they themselves disconcerted.

(xi) It is important that the Senior Officer after addressing the men, should personally retain control of the situation until the men have obeyed orders to disperse or to return to duty.

(xii) A full investigation should be held without delay and a report on the incident forwarded immediately to the Flag or Senior Officer, with the steps proposed to deal adequately with the occurrence.

(xiii) In this connection, attention is drawn to Summary Punishment No. 5: 'Dismissal from H.M. Service' (King's Regulations and Admiralty Instructions, Article 540, Table II), which can be applied with advantage in exceptional cases. Full use should also be made of King's Regulations and Admiralty Instructions, Article 420—'Unsuitable, incompetent and undesirable men'—against whom insufficient evidence can be brought. The approval of the Admiralty or Commander-in-Chief, where necessary in such cases, should be asked for by telegram.

(xiv) The question when and how force should be used must depend on circumstances, but the following general principles should be followed:—

(a) Strong patrols, parties of Petty Officers or loyal ratings, may act as a useful deterrent through a show of force, or as part of any precautionary measures. Such parties, as well as specially selected sentries, may be armed in any manner considered desirable, and if forcibly interfered with in any way or if any attempt is made to prevent their carrying out their duties, they are justified in using force with whatever weapons they are armed.

(*b*) Shooting *to kill* should only be resorted to as a last extremity.

(*c*) In the case of disaffected parties of men who are observing a passive attitude, force should be used to disperse or otherwise deal with them when other means have failed.

(xv) Commanding Officers may be assured of the support of Their Lordships in any proper steps that they may find it necessary to take to deal with an attempt at collective indiscipline.

8. Past experience has shown how important it is that Senior Officers, on whom the responsibility for dealing with insubordination inevitably falls, should be mentally prepared for dealing with an emergency and that they should have an organisation in mind which can be readily brought into action to cope with any situation that might arise. The state of preparedness of the organisation itself must naturally depend upon the Senior Officer's assessment of any degree of tension existing or suspected in the minds of the men under his command.

While it is not necessary for a Commanding Officer to communicate the contents of this document to his subordinates as a matter of course, it is desirable that, when a state of tension exists, that Heads of Departments and possibly other Officers should be taken into confidence in order that the preparedness of the organisation may be advanced to meet the situation, should it deteriorate.

9. In preparing such an organisation the following points should be covered:—

(*a*) The securing of control over vital points, of which malcontents might endeavour to take possession, e.g., small arms stores and racks, keyboards, switchboards, telephone exchange, ship's broadcasting system, bridge and signalling equipment, galleys, etc.

(*b*) The rapid formation of guards and patrols, under picked Officers, Petty Officers and non-commissioned Officers.

(*c*) The provision of arms (both firearms and 'cudgels' of some kind) for these guards and patrols.

(*d*) The establishment of a 'citidel' in a suitable part of the ship, which can be readily defended, to act as a rallying point for loyal elements and a base of operation to regain control of the situation.

10. However serious the situation may appear to be, it can be said with certainty that many of the men can be relied upon, if they are given the proper lead by their Officers and the opportunity to break away from the trouble.

CALENDAR, 1944

	JANUARY	FEBRUARY	MARCH	APRIL
S	2 9 16 23 30	6 13 20 27	5 12 19 26	2 9 16 23 30
M	3 10 17 24 31	7 14 21 28	6 13 20 27	3 10 17 24
Tu	4 11 18 25	1 8 15 22 29	7 14 21 28	4 11 18 25
W	5 12 19 26	2 9 16 23	1 8 15 22 29	5 12 19 26
Th	6 13 20 27	3 10 17 24	2 9 16 23 30	6 13 20 27
F	7 14 21 28	4 11 18 25	3 10 17 24 31	7 14 21 28
S	1 8 15 22 29	5 12 19 26	4 11 18 25	1 8 15 22 29

	MAY	JUNE	JULY	AUGUST
S	7 14 21 28	4 11 18 25	2 9 16 23 30	6 13 20 27
M	1 8 15 22 29	5 12 19 26	3 10 17 24 31	7 14 21 28
Tu	2 9 16 23 30	6 13 20 27	4 11 18 25	1 8 15 22 29
W	3 10 17 24 31	7 14 21 28	5 12 19 26	2 9 16 23 30
Th	4 11 18 25	1 8 15 22 29	6 13 20 27	3 10 17 24 31
F	5 12 19 26	2 9 16 23 30	7 14 21 28	4 11 18 25
S	6 13 20 27	3 10 17 24	1 8 15 22 29	5 12 19 26

	SEPTEMBER	OCTOBER	NOVEMBER	DECEMBER
S	3 10 17 24	1 8 15 22 29	5 12 19 26	3 10 17 24 31
M	4 11 18 25	2 9 16 23 30	6 13 20 27	4 11 18 25
Tu	5 12 19 26	3 10 17 24 31	7 14 21 28	5 12 19 26
W	6 13 20 27	4 11 18 25	1 8 15 22 29	6 13 20 27
Th	7 14 21 28	5 12 19 26	2 9 16 23 30	7 14 21 28
F	1 8 15 22 29	6 13 20 27	3 10 17 24	1 8 15 22 29
S	2 9 16 23 30	7 14 21 28	4 11 18 25	2 9 16 23 30

CALENDAR, 1945

	JANUARY	FEBRUARY	MARCH	APRIL
S	7 14 21 28	4 11 18 25	4 11 18 25	1 8 15 22 29
M	1 8 15 22 29	5 12 19 26	5 12 19 26	2 9 16 23 30
Tu	2 9 16 23 30	6 13 20 27	6 13 20 27	3 10 17 24
W	3 10 17 24 31	7 14 21 28	7 14 21 28	4 11 18 25
Th	4 11 18 25	1 8 15 22	1 8 15 22 29	5 12 19 26
F	5 12 19 26	2 9 16 23	2 9 16 23 30	6 13 20 27
S	6 13 20 27	3 10 17 24	3 10 17 24 31	7 14 21 28

	MAY	JUNE	JULY	AUGUST
S	6 13 20 27	3 10 17 24	1 8 15 22 29	5 12 19 26
M	7 14 21 28	4 11 18 25	2 9 16 23 30	6 13 20 27
Tu	1 8 15 22 29	5 12 19 26	3 10 17 24 31	7 14 21 28
W	2 9 16 23 30	6 13 20 27	4 11 18 25	1 8 15 22 29
Th	3 10 17 24 31	7 14 21 28	5 12 19 26	2 9 16 23 30
F	4 11 18 25	1 8 15 22 29	6 13 20 27	3 10 17 24 31
S	5 12 19 26	2 9 16 23 30	7 14 21 28	4 11 18 25

	SEPTEMBER	OCTOBER	NOVEMBER	DECEMBER
S	2 9 16 23 30	7 14 21 28	4 11 18 25	2 9 16 23 30
M	3 10 17 24	1 8 15 22 29	5 12 19 26	3 10 17 24 31
Tu	4 11 18 25	2 9 16 23 30	6 13 20 27	4 11 18 25
W	5 12 19 26	3 10 17 24 31	7 14 21 28	5 12 19 26
Th	6 13 20 27	4 11 18 25	1 8 15 22 29	6 13 20 27
F	7 14 21 28	5 12 19 26	2 9 16 23 30	7 14 21 28
S	1 8 15 22 29	6 13 20 27	3 10 17 24	1 8 15 22 29

GLOSSARY
of Acronyms

See also pp 35-6, 40, 47

AB	Able seaman	**Lieut, Lt**	Lieutenant
ACI	Atlantic Convoy Instructions	**LMT**	Local mean time
		L Sea or LS	Leading seaman
AFO	Admiralty Fleet Order	**MHS**	Medical history sheet
BR	Book of reference	**MRC**	Medical Research Council
CAFO	Confidential Admiralty Fleet Order	**MTB**	Motor torpedo boat
CB	Confidential book, to be destroyed if in danger of capture	**N**	North
		NDA	Naval Discipline Act
		NM & ER	Naval Magazine and Explosives Regulations
C in C	Commander in chief	**OOD**	Officer of the day
CO	Commanding officer, eg captain of a ship	**OOW**	Officer of the watch
		Ord Sea	Ordinary Seaman
CPO	Chief petty officer	**OU**	Official use, an earlier term for BR
CS	Continuous service		
DF	Direction finding, by radio	**PMO**	Principal medical officer
DR	Dead reckoning	**PO**	Petty officer
D/S	Distributing station	**RDF**	Radio direction finding, an early term for radar
DTM	Destroyer Technical Manual		
DTO	Destroyers Tactical and Technical Orders	**Revs**	Revolutions
		RFR	Royal Fleet Reserve – made up of retired naval seamen
E	East		
EP	Estimated position		
ER	Engine room	**RNH**	Royal Naval Hospital
ET	Educational test	**RNR**	Royal Naval Reserve – merchant navy seamen
FAP	First aid post		
GCB	Good conduct badge	**RNVR**	Royal Naval Volunteer
GMT	Greenwich Mean Time	**Reserve**	Non-seamen
GPO	General Post Office	**S**	South
H, HF	Home Fleet	**SL**	Sidelight
HA	High angle, ie anti-aircraft	**SMG**	Speed made good
HMML	His Majesty's Motor Launch	**SS**	Short service
HMMTB	His Majesty's Motor Torpedo Boat	**Sub-Lieut**	Sub-lieutenant
		V/S	Visual signalling
HMS	His Majesty's Ship	**W**	West
HO	Hostilities Only	**WO**	War Office
HWO	Home Fleet War Orders	**WR**	Wardroom
KR & AI	Kings Regulations and Admiralty Instructions	**W/T**	Wireless telegraphy
		ZT	Zone time
LA	Low angle		

INDEX

ACKNOWLEDGEMENTS & REFERENCES

All images reproduced here are from the original documents issued to British naval officers during the years 1939 to 1945, and from contemporary books. The author and publisher would like to thank Val Biro for the use of illustrations from *Roll on My Twelve* (on pages 45, 76, 86, 102, 129); Lady Pamela and Alan Macdonald for the use of Sir Roderick Macdonald's illustrations from *The Figurehead* (on pages 22, 47, 89, 93, 114); Stephen Dent for plans on final endpapers and pages 63, 74, 87; Roger Furse for illustrations on pages 82, 88, 97, 107, 132, 134; and John Worsley for those on pages 26, 83 and 91. Anova Books Ltd is committed to respecting the intellectual property rights of others. We have therefore taken all reasonable efforts to ensure that the reproduction of all images is done with the full consent of the copyright holders. If you are aware of any unintentional omissions, please contact the company so that any necessary corrections may be made for future editions.

Printed books: David Bolster, *Roll on My Twelve* (1945); Frank Carr, *The Yacht Masters Guide* (London, 1943); John Fernald, *Destroyer from America* (London, 1942); *First Aid in the Royal Navy* (London, 1943); Alec Guinness, *Blessings in Disguise* (London, 1985); *The Gunnery Pocket Book* (London, 1943); J Lennox Kerr and Wilfred Granville, *The RNVR* (London, 1957); *King Alfred magazine* (Vol 1. nos 1–12, May 1940 – May/June 1941); Brian Lavery, *Churchill's Navy* (London, 2006); Brian Lavery, *River-Class Frigates and the Battle of the Atlantic* (London, 2006); Sir Roderick Macdonald, *The Figurehead* (Bishop Auckland, 1993); David Putt, *Men Dressed as Seamen* (London, 1943); R Ransome Wallis, *Two Red Stripes* (Shepperton, 1993); Joseph Wellings, *On His Majesty's Service* (Newport, Rhode Island, 1983).

Source material: National Archives Adm 1/15676, 1/18952, 1/18958, 1/22967, 182/110, 234/146, 234/290; National Maritime Museum, GTN5/7.

Conway, an imprint of Bloomsbury Publishing Plc
50 Bedford Square, London WC1B 3DP
www.bloomsbury.com

Compilation and Introduction © Brian Lavery 2007
Volume © Conway 2007

First published by Anova Books Ltd 2007
First Bloomsbury edition 2015

ISBN 978-1-8448-6054-8

A CIP catalogue record for this book is available from the British Library.

Printed and bound in Great Britain by CPI Group (UK) Ltd, Croydon CR0 4YY